GUILT:

ISSUES OF EMOTIONAL LIVING
IN AN AGE OF STRESS
FOR CLERGY AND RELIGIOUS

GUILT:

ISSUES OF EMOTIONAL LIVING
IN AN AGE OF STRESS
FOR CLERGY AND RELIGIOUS

THE FIFTH
PSYCHOTHEOLOGICAL SYMPOSIUM

PHILOMENA AGUDO

BERNARD J. BUSH

SEAN D. SAMMON

KATHLEEN E. KELLEY

VINCENT M. BILOTTA III

JOSEPH L. HART

E. J. FRANASIAK

Edited by Kathleen E. Kelley

With a Foreword by Thomas A. Kane

AFFIRMATION BOOKS

WHITINSVILLE, MASSACHUSETTS

PUBLISHED WITH ECCLESIASTICAL PERMISSION

First Edition

©1980 by House of Affirmation, Inc.

Library of Congress Cataloging in Publication Data
Psychotheological Symposium, 5th, Aquinas Junior College, etc., 1979.
  Guilt, issues of emotional living in an age of stress for clergy and religious.
    1. Catholic Church—Clergy—Psychology—Congresses.
  2. Monastic and religious life—Psychology—Congresses.

ISBN 0-89571-008-0

Printed by Mercantile Printing Company, Worcester, MA
United States of America

To

present and former residents
of the House of Affirmation
with love and gratitude

AFFIRMATION BOOKS is an important part of the ministry of the House of Affirmation, International Therapeutic Center for Clergy and Religious, founded by Sr. Anna Polcino, S.C.M.M., M.D.

CONTENTS

FOREWORD

Some years ago, I noted that, from a psychotheological viewpoint, the new catechetical movement was carelessly addressing the issue of guilt, or, in some instances, completely doing away with it. I was often criticized for this position. I could understand what I considered an over-reaction to my remarks because of the obvious fact that much Christian doctrine in the past had produced an enormous number of guilt-ridden persons. This evidence suggested that the catechetical movement had been influenced by some psychotherapeutic schools that viewed all guilt as symptomatic of illness.

There is no doubt that false guilt is an enemy of peace. However, true guilt helps us to be consciously aware of our behavior and of our personal responsibility for that behavior. Not to consider guilt as healthy could lead to generations of sociopaths. In addition, feelings of guilt help us to understand that our behavior results from choices that could be sinful, and not just from involuntary sickness.

This present book, *Guilt: Issues of Emotional Living in an Age of Stress for Clergy and Religious,* offers an interesting group of essays that are not intended to be decisive conclusions, but which can serve as instruments to lead the reader to further personal reflection and academic investigation of the subject matter. As a psychotherapist who has limited his practice to clergypersons for over ten years, I am certainly aware that unhealthy guilt is, unhappily, very common among ministers of the Gospel. These persons are meant to be peacemakers, but they know very little personal peace.

I believe these essays by my colleagues at the various centers of our House of Affirmation family will be helpful to those who suffer from excessive guilt, and who desire to feel the healing which Jesus Himself has promised to His followers.

> Peace is my farewell to you, my peace is my gift to you; I do not give it to you as the world gives peace. Do not be distressed or fearful. (John 14:27)

Sister Kathleen E. Kelley, S. N. D., is the editor of this book. Sister Kathleen, affectionately called Sister Katie by those of us who know her well, is the founding director of our House of Affirmation in Webster Groves, Missouri. As pastor of our Affirmation family in Webster Groves, Sister Katie has as her mandate to preserve the spiritual values and to guide the scientific concerns of our House of Affirmation psychotheological residential therapeutic community there. Readers of this book will come to know something of this woman of faith and woman of science as they read Sister Katie's introduction and essay, as well as the other essays she has gathered and edited for this volume. She is a special gift of God to our House of Affirmation family, and we are happy to share her insights with our friends.

Affirmation Books has grown tremendously since its founding in 1976. We hope that this present volume receives the enthusiastic response of our previous publications. During the coming years, we promise you many more Affirmation Books that will, hopefully, challenge your thought and encourage your faith.

Thomas A. Kane, Ph.D., D.P.S.
Priest, Diocese of Worcester
Publisher, Affirmation Books
Whitinsville, Massachusetts

January 7, 1980

PREFACE

The fifth psychotheological symposium sponsored by the House of Affirmation, International Therapeutic Center for Clergy and Religious, brought together in October and November, 1979, over 1600 people in Boston, Massachusetts, San Francisco, California, and St. Louis, Missouri, to explore the experience of guilt. The attendance at this symposium suggests the earnest struggle in which men and women engage on a personal level when dealing with the guilt experiences inherent in their lives. Because of the interest in this topic, we offer our symposium presentations in published form as we have in the past, both as a service to those who were unable to attend one of these sessions, and as a source of continued reflection for those who were present.

The essays in this volume deal with: the guilt experience as it affects our growth toward responsibility and wholeness as Christians; unhealthy or neurotic guilt in terms of its origin and of its impact on an individual's response to life; the area of Christian conscience and the role that the expectations of others have in its development; the impact of the mid-life transitional experience; and guilt as a creative force in our lives. In addition to the essays presented at the symposium, two papers written especially for this publication are included. One deals with the origin of guilt feelings and our use of them; and the other, with guilt in relation to personal responsibility and affirmed sufficiency.

The topic guilt presents a complex area for exploration. Because religious tradition, family, and culture are the major contributors to the guilt phenomenon, our experience of these areas shapes our understanding of guilt and gives it both its commonality and its uniqueness. The guilt experience, then, is familiar to all of us, and we all seek ways to deal with it.

Many recent books offer quick remedies for handling these feelings of guilt, but their authors view guilt primarily from a negative viewpoint. Christianity offers an understanding of guilt as a potentially creative life force that calls us to more honest, more authentic relationships with God, with ourselves, and with others.

These annual symposiums have made it clear that many people are seeking a better understanding of themselves through the integration of psychological development and theological truth. The guilt experience is one that can damage us psychologically and diminish us theologically if the positive and life-giving dimensions of it are lost to the superficial answers that are promoted by some writers.

Our work at the House of Affirmation has shown us that the experience of church and family can be felt as negative and detrimental to the full response asked of us as

Christians. The thrust of our work is to help people to look at their histories, to take seriously their experiences, and to cope more effectively with the demands of being responsible human beings. This challenge is part of the process of healing and reconciliation that is the saving message of the Lord.

Many hands joined together to prepare for the symposium, and to these people I offer a word of special thanks. In continued support of our work, the Sisters of Saint Joseph at Aquinas Junior College in Newton again extended their gracious hospitality. In San Francisco, the Sisters of the Presentation opened their facility for our use; and in St. Louis, the staff at St. John's Mercy Hospital welcomed us. The moderators of the symposium, Rev. Thomas A. Kane (St. Louis), Sr. Anna Polcino (San Francisco), and Bro. Sean Sammon (Boston), and the generous staff members at each center of the House of Affirmation gave time and personal support to handle the organizational details necessary to make the days run smoothly. Finally, I thank the writers whose articles appear in this book for sharing themselves and their insights.

At each center, the symposium is part of our "Affirmation" weekend when we welcome back former residents from their ministries throughout the country. We cherish the memory of all those who came to Whitinsville and Montara and Webster Groves in 1979 as we consider their courage to go on risking life, and we continue to value the significant contributions and gracious presence of our present residents.

Kathlen E. Kelley, S.N.D.
House of Affirmation
Webster Groves, Missouri

Sister Philomena Agudo, F.M.M., Ph.D., is a full-time psychotherapist at the House of Affirmation in Whitinsville, Massachusetts. A member of the Franciscan Missionaries of Mary, Sister Agudo received her undergraduate and early graduate education in her native country, the Philippines, at Our Lady of Loretto College and at Ateneo University. She received her doctorate in pastoral psychology and counseling from Boston University. Before joining the staff of the House of Affirmation, she was a staff member at Boston's South End Center for Alcoholism, at Lemuel Shattuck Hospital with terminal cancer patients, and at the Danielson Counseling Center, Boston University. Before coming to the United States, she served as a missionary in Indonesia and Singapore.

GUILT: ITS EFFECT ON WHOLENESS

Philomena Agudo

Guilt is a human phenomenon. It could be an anxiety-provoking thorn in one's psyche, or it could also be a growth-stimulating element in one's personality. There is in every person an automatic self-evaluator. Freud calls it the superego; for us, it is conscience. Guilt is a mental process rather than a feeling. It is the process of judging or condemning one's behavior, thoughts, or words. This process automatically produces feelings of shame and grief. These feelings motivate and regulate the individual's response to his/her impulses, a condition which eventually contributes to the development of the individual's personality. Shame is the feeling evoked after the individual had interiorly made a judgment of the self's violation of a standard value or norm of conduct. As Lewis states:

> Shame is a "painful emotion"...; guilt may or may not

be accompanied by affect. Shame thus involves more of an affective component awareness than guilt.[1]

Guilt also produces a sense of grief or "loss." The awareness of the transgression brings about shame which in turn results in a loss of self-esteem. This loss of self-esteem could also generate fear of losing a love object whom the individual wants to please. This loss is the hardest blow that guilt deals a person.

THE CONCEPT OF "WHOLENESS"

Before I can touch on the effects of guilt upon the individual, I would like first to clarify my concept of "wholeness" of personality. I refer to "wholeness" as the harmonious unification or integration of the physiological, psychological, and spiritual elements that make up a human person. "Wholeness" also presupposes that the individual undergoes or is undergoing the process of growth and integration as manifested in his/her capacity to love the self and others, to enjoy a sense of self-confidence and security, to affirm reality in daily life, to cope effectively with the painful and unpleasant, as well as the capacity to be grateful for and to enjoy the blessings that accompany our human existence. The term "wholeness" is relative. There is no such state as "perfect wholeness." All of us are striving toward that wholeness, and each one varies in his/her degree of wholeness. St. Paul must have been aware of what "wholeness" means when he exhorted Timothy in one of his letters to "Strive for righteousness, godliness, faith, love, endurance and gentleness" (I Tim. 6:11).

---

1. Helen B. Lewis, *Shame and Guilt in Neurosis* (New York: International University Press, Inc., 1971), p. 85.

Wholeness further involves the awareness that what affects the individual psychologically has repercussions on the body as well as on relationships—with God and others. Wholeness is possible only because the individual values himself/herself. It is the appreciation and gratitude for one's existence, one's potential and gifts, limitations included, that the individual is motivated to maintain continually that physiological, psychological, and spiritual health necessary to continue the process of growth and integration.

ABSENCE OF GUILT

Because of that power within us to evaluate the self according to our internalized standards and values, guilt will always have an impact on our personality. Even the unawareness of guilt affects the individual's personality. It is the sociopath who is insensitive to guilt. The sociopath, formerly known as psychopath, is the "antisocial personality." Bowman describes this personality:

> This term is reserved for individuals who are basically unsocialized and whose behavior pattern brings them repeatedly into conflict with society. They are incapable of significant loyalty to individuals, groups or social values. They are grossly selfish, callous, irresponsible, impulsive, and unable to feel guilt or to learn from experience and punishment. . . .[2]
>
> . . . .
>
> Psychopathic antisocial behavior is at once biologic and social, a product of constitution and heredity and experience.[3]

---

2. Bolman Wolman, *The Therapist's Handbook* (New York: Van Nostrand Reinhold Co., 1976), pp. 414-15.
3. Ibid., p. 417.

The sociopath is unable to listen to that "self-evaluator" called conscience. This inability to be aware of his/her guilt and to feel shame, remorse, or grief produces patterns of behavior that are self-defeating and destructive. Needless to say, the inability to be aware of one's guilt, of transgressing an established value or norm of behavior, incapacitates one from entering into the process of growth and integration.

GUILT-AWARENESS

To be aware of one's guilt is to confirm one's adherence to a value system and acceptable social norms. Guilt awareness brings the individual into a realistic confrontation of one's human fallibility. The quality of one's growth and personality integration is measurable through one's ability to deal with one's awareness of a personal transgression of a commitment to a value system.

The conscience performs a monitoring function to the self. Just as persistent physical pain is a bodily signal that there is something malfunctioning among the organs, guilt is triggered by the conscience to give the signal of a transgression or a violation. The feelings of shame and loss of self-esteem could influence the individual in his/her manner of dealing with guilt. Peter and Judas differed very greatly in dealing with the painful reality of guilt. While one was healing and integrating, the other was self-defeating and destructive. What influences the individual's manner of handling guilt? Why are some persons destructive in coping with their guilt, whereas some are able to use it as a means of growth and integration?

The answers to these questions are derived from two kinds of guilt, the neurotic and the real.

NEUROTIC GUILT

Neurotic guilt has its roots in childhood:

It will be remembered that the child requires security. If he is denied security, he becomes anxious and the behavior to which he turns to reduce the anxiety will become fixated through the functioning of the law of effect. If the child experiences reward and punishment in approximately equal amounts at the hands of his parents, he is likely to become confused concerning his relationship with them. He feels insecure because their reaction to what he does is likely to be wrath as love. He is emotionally dependent upon them, but he never knows when they will support him or when they will reject him. The situation is especially chaotic for the child when the reward or punishment comes many hours, or perhaps many days, after the behavioral act. An erratic pattern in the distribution of love and wrath is very disturbing for the child. In such a situation he learns anxiety, and the anxiety in turn, is likely to be accompanied by a feeling of guilt.[4]

The development of neurotic guilt is further reinforced in school where the child is expected to behave as an adult and God is presented as a punishing tyrant. If this child happens to decide on being a priest or religious, the negative quality of religious formation would complete the transformation into a full-blown neurotic.

THE EFFECTS OF NEUROTIC GUILT

Neurotic guilt fractures the personality and inhibits the process of growth and integration through the following destructive behavioral patterns:

1. Self-rejection
2. Hostility

---

4. Hebert Carroll, *Mental Hygiene: The Dynamics of Adjustment* (New Jersey: Prentice Hall Inc., 1956), p. 172.

3. Paranoidal ideation

4. Depression due to nagging anxiety

The destructive patterns affect not only the individual but also his/her relationship to others and to God. The quality of his/her relationships also possesses some tinge of destructiveness.

1. Self-rejection

Neurotic guilt has no room for compassion. The individual is immersed in shame and anger over the transgression. The anger is turned toward the self. Just as the neurotic had experienced the wrath or fury of a punitive parent, that same wrath is perpetuated, only this time, not by the parent but by the individual himself/herself. This anger toward the self consequently brings about the rejection of oneself. The person who rejects himself/herself has already depreciated his/her self-worth. Guilt-awareness also brings with it an unconscious self-hate:

> Since the patient unconsciously hates himself, he is justified in saying that he feels unloved and unlovable. He also realizes that he does not feel the love for others. . . . Neurotically depressed persons usually go further than this; they behave cruelly to those whom they would like to love and go on loving. If, as a result, they suffer from remorse, the remorse is fully justified. Each curt answer or sharp protest, each temper outburst, each quarrel leads to an increase in realistic guilt; and each increase in realistic guilt brings an increase in the hostility of the archaic superego.[5]

2. Hostility

Since the individual has condemned the self, there is hostility directed toward the self as well as toward others.

5. Norman Cameron, *Personality Development and Psychopathology* (Boston: Houghton Mifflin Co., 1963), p. 419.

One can only give to others what one has. If the person bears hostile feelings toward himself/herself, the very same feelings are transferred to others. The guilt-ridden individual is judgmental of others because of the hostility within. He/she condemns others for what the self has condemned in himself/herself. As Lewis explains:

> The position of the self as the initiator of guilt, and the determiner or judge of extent of responsibility, puts the self "in charge" of the hostility directed against itself. It also puts the self in charge of the distribution of hostility. . . .
>
> . . . .
>
> Similarly, the active role of the self in guilt makes it possible that hostility is discharged upon "others" as well as upon the self, thereby creating an affinity between guilt and projection of hostility.[6]

3. Paranoidal Ideation

Neurotic guilt drives the individual into being "suspicious" of others. Because the individual hates himself/herself and considers his/her worthlessness to be real, he/she also suspects that others, even loved ones, can feel nothing but hatred and contempt for his/her worthlessness. It becomes impossible to accept or to believe in other people's appreciation or affirmation. This paranoidal ideation in turn brings about the destruction of relationships which are valuable to the individual. Projected hostility breeds hostility in return, and the individual suffering from neurotic guilt finds himself/herself isolated. According to Lewis:

> "Hostile Belligerence" is characterized by a complaining attitude, manifest hostility and an inclination to ex-

---

6. Helen B. Lewis, *Shame and Guilt in Neurosis,* pp. 44-45.

press resentment towards others, and to feel suspicious of the intentions of others. . . . Those who are guilt-prone demonstrate by finding fault with the people and circumstances around them.[7]

4. Depression Due to Anxiety

Because of the intense anxiety created by guilt, the individual may develop some kind of phobia. There are times when both anxiety and unconscious shame result in depression. The anxiety oftentimes is due to the unconscious fear of punishment. The onslaught of that "floating anxiety" as well as the ever-pervasive loss of self-esteem drags the individual into the pit of depression:

> . . . worry thoughts may appear under the influence of an unconscious state of guilt or responsibility. Or the self may occur in the wake of by-passed shame—feeling. Similarly, depressed mood may be instated without the person's awareness that he is coping with shame feeling. Moreover, the superego can operate with varying patterns of awareness which seem to differ with individual personality. Less differentiated patients often experience the operation of the superego as shame, i.e., with particular awareness of the "other" devaluing the self. These patients also have a higher level of negative affect which they experience as depression.[8]

Neurotic guilt incapacitates the individual from loving and receiving love. He/she cannot be compassionate to the self nor to others. The fractured personality is unable to relate effectively to others or to God. Feelings of hostility block the individual's sensitivity to those who reach out to him/her in love. This very same hostility blocks the awareness of the gentle touch of God's grace; furthermore,

---

7. Ibid., p. 140.
8. Ibid., p. 28.

it blinds the individual to the reality of God's unconditional compassion.

How does one cope with neurotic guilt? Since neurotic guilt is rooted in a stunted or malformed personality, there is no magic formula. The fixations, emotional distress, and unresolved conflicts involved necessitate a therapeutic process that can facilitate the continuance of emotional growth and healing. To refuse to seek professional help in coping with neurotic guilt would expose one to an interminable and unbearable torment. Shakespeare might have had such guilt in mind when he wrote, "Those whose guilt within their bosom lies, imagine every eye beholds their blame."

REAL GUILT

"Guilt is the free decision to evil, evil with regard to God and man."[9] Real guilt presupposes a healthy conscience, a healthy "self-evaluator" that perceives one's motives and actions accurately. It also presupposes that the individual is totally free to make a decision. If we look at our moral values (commandments and precepts) as a means by which that Supreme Authority—God—protects us from self-destruction and the destruction of others, then real guilt involves a conscious and a free decision to break a Significant Relationship rather than a mere violation of imposed moral standards. Real guilt, therefore, also presupposes the individual's awareness and capacity to "relate" to the Significant Being who is the source of one's moral values.

Authentic guilt is the conscious awareness of one's free choice of a behavior that is destructive to oneself as well as to others. It is, in fact, a free act of rejection of a Signifi-

9. Karl Rahner, Cornelius Ernst, Kevin Smyth et al., ed., *Sacramentum Mundi* (New York: Herder and Herder, 1970), p. 89.

cant Relationship (moral source), of oneself, and of others due to the free choice of what is evil and destructive. It is the realization of one's choice of *rejection and destruction* that produces feelings of remorse rather than the fear of punishment or shame. Remorse is possible only because the individual fully appreciates the relationship established with the Supreme Being who is the source of his/her morality. It takes a mature and responsible individual to be capable of the feeling of remorse because it is a painful feeling of regret, a feeling of compunction, a full acceptance of responsibility for the act. Authentic guilt does not drag the individual into despair or self-hatred because the individual's Significant Relationship is based on love, trust, and compassion. The individual is able to face and to accept guilt because he/she is aware of the availability of reconciliation and his/her reinstatement into that Significant Relationship of love, trust, and compassion. The feeling of remorse in real guilt is akin to the feeling of grief— sorrow over the loss of a special relationship as well as the loss of one's integrity. This grief, however, is not adulterated with bitterness or the fear of punishment. The individual is aware of his/her fallibility and has accepted it. He/she with all the good will to remain "just" is fully aware that there is the possibility of "falling" more than "seven times" daily. The acceptance of human weakness opens the individual to compassion with himself/herself and others. The acceptance of human weakness does not mean giving in to permissiveness. The mature and responsible individual is fully conscious of the reality that despite the limitations of human nature, barring brain dysfunction, each one is capable of making choices. Each one is free to use or abuse God's gifts. Sixteen centuries ago, St.

John Chrysostom expounded this truth which is still applicable to our time:

> When these deplorable excesses happen many cry out: "Would there were no wine!" What folly! What madness! Men sin, and you straightway find fault with the gifts of God! It is utter lunacy! Is it the wine that causes this abuse? Of course not; it is the intemperance of those who take a wrong delight in it. . . . Wine was given to us that it might be a source of delight, not that we might dishonor ourselves. . . . God honored us with the gift; why do we dishonor ourselves by abusing it?[10]

THE MAIN DIFFERENCES BETWEEN REAL GUILT AND NEUROTIC GUILT

1. Real guilt is based on a conscious and free act, whereas neurotic guilt is influenced by an unconscious pattern of guilt which has its roots in childhood.

2. Real guilt stimulates compunction and a desire for reconciliation with a Significant Relationship—the source of moral values, whereas neurotic guilt produces shame, anger, and hostility. Neurotic guilt directs anger and hatred toward the source of morality.

3. Real guilt does not inhibit hope, love, and trust because of the individual's capacity to accept compassion. Neurotic guilt pushes the individual to despair. He/she is incapable of compassion or forgiveness and is therefore unable to accept forgiveness or compassion from anyone.

4. Real guilt is deliberate; neurotic guilt is compulsive. In real guilt, the individual is fully aware of his/her responsibility in the choice of a particular act, whereas the neurotic's compulsive behavior lessens conscious responsibility.

---

10. Donald Atwater, *St. John Chrysostom: The Voice of Gold* (Milwaukee: The Bruce Publishing Co., 1939), p. 54.

EFFECTS OF THE ACCEPTANCE OF REAL GUILT

1. Self-Honesty

Awareness of one's real guilt is an honest acceptance of one's fallibility. It is self-honesty that brings forth an accurate perception of one's potential to be whole as well as one's imperfection. Self-honesty breeds both self-confidence and humility. St. Teresa of Avila expressed such self-honesty when she wrote in her autobiography:

> O my Jesus! What a sight it is when you through your mercy return to offer Your hand and raise up a soul that has fallen in sin...! How such a soul knows the multitude of Your grandeurs and mercies and its own misery! In this state it is in truth consumed and knows your splendors. Here it doesn't dare raise its eyes, and here it raises them up so as to know what it owes You.[11]

2. Emotional Growth

In accepting one's guilt, one is able to be in touch with sorrow and compunction. Working through these feelings stimulates the intense desire for forgiveness and reconciliation which restore peace and emotional equilibrium in the individual. Every time the individual receives the sign of forgiveness and reconciliation through the sacrament of penance, he/she experiences a "call" to growth towards emotional and spiritual maturity. This "call" to growth is clearly seen in the lives of St. Augustine, St. Margaret of Cortona, as well as Charles de Foucauld, the founder of the Little Brothers of Jesus.

3. Restoration of Self-Esteem

When the individual is able to accept fully forgiveness and compassion, he/she experiences the restoration of

11. St. Teresa of Avila, *Collected Works,* vol. 1, trans. Kiernan Kavanaugh, O.C.D., and Otilio Rodriquez, O.C.D. (Washington, DC: I.C.S. Publications, 1976), p. 124.

his/her self-esteem. To be forgiven means to be reconciled. Reconciliation is actually the re-affirmation of the person. The Gospels relate how Christ's look of compassion and forgiveness lifted Mary Magdalen and Peter from painful remorse to a degree of self-esteem which enabled them to take risks in relation to Him.

In the sacrament of reconciliation, we presuppose that the repentant individual is fully aware of human weakness and accepts the reality of human propensity to transgress moral law because of this weakness. However, the truly repentant despite the remorse continues to trust in that unconditional re-affirmation from both God and fellow-beings. The sacrament of reconciliation is a sign of the individual's being re-affirmed by God through the words pronounced by His representative. The words "I forgive you. . . ." imply that the reality of human weakness is understood and that divine and human compassion can bring about a spiritual healing by re-affirming the individual, the inevitable effect of which is the restoration of the individual's self-esteem.

4. Strengthens the Ego

The sense of being forgiven and reconciled produces a sense of security. Reconciliation with God means the restoration and reinforcement of grace. When one fully believes that God is present in one's whole being, then he/she can say with St. John Chrysostom:

> Christ is with me; what then have I to fear? The floods of the seas and the rage of the princes of this world put together can do me no more harm than a spider's web. . . . If it be God's will that this thing should happen, let it happen.[12]

---

12. Donald Attwater, *St. John Chrysostom,* p. 126.

5. Reinforces the Capacity to Be Compassionate

The repetition of a particular experience is eventually internalized by the individual and becomes a part of his personality. Repeated signs of mercy and forgiveness which the individual receives through the sacrament of reconciliation eventually turn him/her to being a compassionate person not only toward others, but especially toward himself/herself. Pope John XXIII is universally loved especially because of his compassionate understanding of human behavior. He was the first pope who did not issue any encyclical of condemnation. It was his compassion that enabled him to cope with dissensions during Vatican II.

> In the course of the first session of the Council it was plain that the majority of the bishops and cardinals did not agree with the ultra-conservative position of Cardinal Ottaviani. Cardinal Ottaviani was particularly displeased with the debate on the proposal entitled "The Sources of Revelation." He went to Pope John and complained about dissension and indicated that a quiet word from the Pope could put an end to further dissension and discussion. John is reported to have said, "Dissension? Don't you remember that at the Council of Trent one Italian Bishop tore the beard off a Greek Bishop?" Ottaviani hinted that if the arguments continued he might resign to avoid affronts to his dignity. Pope John quietly replied, "You will stay. There will be no resignation."[13]

CONCLUSION

Reflecting on the implications of guilt upon our daily life, we need to address ourselves to some questions:

---

13. Louis Michaels, *The Humor and Warmth of Pope John XXIII,* (New York: Pocket Books Inc., 1965), pp. 70-71.

1. How do we perceive guilt? Do we accept it as a normal human phenomenon, or do we fight it endlessly by building walls of defenses and putting on layers of masks in the effort to hide it?

2. With what kind of guilt are we in touch within the self? If it is neurotic guilt, what have we done about it? If it is real guilt, have we used it to bring forth wholeness in our personality?

3. Unconsciously, what kind of guilt do we stir up among those to whom we minister? How do we cope with persons who try to manipulate us through guilt?

4. Where are we in compassion
   —toward self?
   —toward others?

The experiences of guilt in our lifetime bring with them both torment and blessing. Each one of us has the power to choose. The psalmist chose and expresses this choice so beautifully:

> You, Lord, are all I have,
>   and you give me all I need;
>   my life is in your hands.
> How wonderful are your gifts to me;
>   how good they are!
>
> I praise the Lord, because he guides me,
>   and in the night my conscience warns me.
>
> I am always aware of the Lord's presence;
>   he is near, and nothing can shake me.
>
> And so I am full of happiness and joy,
>   and I always feel secure;
>   because you will not allow me to go to the
>   world of the dead,
>   you will not abandon to the depths below
>   the one you love.

You will show me the path that leads to life;
　your presence fills me with joy,
　and your help brings pleasure forever.

(Ps. 16: 5-11)

What is your choice?

Reverend Bernard J. Bush, S.J., M.A., S.T.M., is director of the House of Affirmation in Montara, California. A member of the California Province of the Society of Jesus who was ordained in 1965, Father Bush studied theology at Regis College, Willowdale, Ontario. He served as student chaplain at the University of San Francisco before assuming the post of spiritual director at the Jesuit theologate in Berkeley, California. From there he went to Boston State Hospital where he interned in pastoral psychology. In 1974 he joined the staff of the House of Affirmation and opened its Boston office. Father Bush has written numerous articles concerning spirituality and social justice, most notably in *The Way*. He has been active in the directed retreat movement and has lectured on Ignatian spirituality, religious life, mental health, and social justice.

THE CRITICAL EYE

Bernard J. Bush

The information that comes to us from people who are knowledgeable in such matters indicates that the feelings which we associate with guilt are common to all cultures and ages. It appears that even humanity in its early stages suffered from the experience. In an era when people felt a causal connection between personal behavior and environmental consequences, guilt feelings were quite profound and very mysterious. Every time there was a flood, earthquake, eclipse, drought, disease, or unusual occurrence, there would be much soul-searching. The cause of something going wrong outside would be sought inside. There is still a great deal of this consciousness with us today.

UNIVERSAL EXPERIENCE OF GUILT

While we may assert that guilt is a universal human experience, we are often hard pressed to define it or to describe it accurately. Guilt appears to be a combination of feelings rather than one simple feeling. Some of its elements seem to be fear, shame, and anxiety. The fear component is related to the expectation of punishment for some real or imagined wrong doing. Shame appears to be related to disappointing someone or not living up to the expectations of others. Anxiety has many dimensions, but it would appear that the anxiety in guilt is associated with a sense that something is wrong or amiss. This anxiety can be due to a sense that I said the wrong thing, am in the wrong place, or did something wrong. In any case, there is a feeling that something is dreadfully out of harmony.

The intensity of guilt feelings, as well as what triggers a reaction of guilt, varies from person to person. In fact, guilt feelings are quite elusive; they sometimes appear very strong and at other times not, even within the same person in comparable circumstances. On one occasion, a child's complaint may bring on intense guilt in a parent, while the same complaint at another time will not. As we know from experience, however, guilt is quite easy to induce in others. In fact, it is impossible to avoid completely even doing or saying things that will make another person feel guilty.

The feeling of guilt occurs most commonly when a person acts, thinks, or speaks in violation of a personal obligation. The problem is compounded because oftentimes the person is not even aware of the obligation until guilt strikes. Some time ago, there was circulating a cartoon which showed a psychiatrist speaking to his patient who was, of course, lying on a couch. The psychiatrist said, "Wilkes, are you still feeling guilty after all this time in therapy? You should be ashamed!"

Here we have a sample of "laying a guilt trip" and the fact that it is possible to feel guilty about feeling guilty. In the cartoon cited, the patient probably was not aware that he had an obligation not to disappoint his therapist until he felt guilty about it. We frequently do the same kinds of things to one another. Thus the response of guilt feelings occurs around the "oughts," "shoulds," "musts," and "supposed tos" in our lives. They are so pervasive and are such a problem in counseling that in my office I have a sign that reads, "Give up 'oughts' all you who enter here." It does not work, of course, but it serves as a good reminder.

THE CRITICAL EYE

I have entitled this paper "The Critical Eye" because I believe that the common component of guilt feelings is some kind of consciousness that I am being observed in a judgmental and condemnatory fashion. This observing eye can be either external or internal. In the case of the cartoon cited, the initial eye was external in the person of the therapist. However, the observation would have no power to induce a feeling of guilt were there not a resonance somehow agreeing within. The internal, critical eye is stimulated from outside by a reminder of a deficiency or wrongness. The situation is an example of someone's saying that in his or her estimation I am or did something I was not supposed to be or do. Since I am already predisposed to accept the evaluation, my own internal eye then goes on to judge and punish.

Let us reflect for a moment upon the times we have said yes when we would have preferred to say no, but saying no would make us feel guilty. An example comes to mind of an occasion recently when an angel-faced young boy came to my door and asked me to sponsor him in a walkathon. How could I say no? I do not personally support the cause for which he was walking. Yet the appeal of his cuteness and the list of names of my neighbors who were supporting him induced me to support him. Human respect (what would my neighbors think?) and a fear of disappointing that cute youth led me to do something I ordinarily would not have done. I avoided a pang of guilt. However, the price I paid was anger at myself for allowing myself to be thus manipulated.

Another example of a time recently when my phone rang comes to mind. The charming voice said she was calling on behalf of the San Mateo Sheriff's Benevolent Association and would I care to contribute. My response was an immediate groaning, "Oh, NO!" She asked what was wrong. I said I was in the middle of writing an article, and she was the last person I wanted to hear from. She replied, "I'm sorry for interrupting you," and hung up. This incident is a case where through quick thinking I reversed the situation and laid a guilt trip on her. None of these examples are particularly admirable for their mature and direct communication. If we reflect for a moment on these situations and others that I am sure come to mind, we shall see that many of our interactions revolve around some aspect of guilt or its avoidance.

ORIGIN OF GUILT AND THEOLOGICAL CONSEQUENCES

One widely held theory of the origin of guilt feelings involves what psychology calls the process of introjection. It simply means that infants and children absorb the values and standards of those around them. This absorption is done both consciously and unconsciously. However, it seems that very early a connection between doing the right thing and approval is established. When the child does the wrong thing, approval and perhaps affection are withheld, and even punishment given. This association makes a very deep impression very early, so that injunctions, laws, orders, and even glances of disapproval have a very strong impact. This impression lasts into adult life. The result is that in many people there persists a connection that I am good when I do good and I am bad when I do bad.

Now, of course, it is easy to see how this interior disposition has serious theological consequences. The inner conviction that someone is watching and judging unfavorably easily gets projected onto God. After all, God is the One who sees all and knows all, even our most private thoughts. Moreover, God is the ultimate judge with the direst of sanctions for transgressions. The threat of an extended period in purgatory or an eternity in hell is enough to put fear in the heart of anyone who thinks about it. Additionally, there is the anxiety of never being sure where I stand with God. We have been taught as an integral part of our theology that it is impossible to know if we are in the state of grace. The result of such theology in the case of people who are already predisposed to be nervous about such things—and who is not?—is to produce a kind of background sense of guilt.

Unfortunately, it frequently happens that this image of God as punitive eye-in-the-sky becomes the focal point of our relationship with Him. God is seen as the avenger for wrongdoing, and, moreover, as unpredictable and capricious. This God must be propitiated and His negative judgments and reactions forestalled. At the very best, such an attitude produces a cautious approach to life and spiritual mediocrity.

GUILT AND MORAL JUDGMENT

Since our feelings of guilt are themselves capricious and unpredictable, it is easy to see how they can warp and distort true moral judgment. The presence and intensity of the feelings tend to preoccupy and distract our attention so that the use of reason and judgment is impaired. The feelings of guilt in themselves are not an accurate gauge of the goodness or badness, the virtue or the vice, of our actions. The presence or absence of guilt does not say anything about our state of grace.

First of all, the reference point of guilt feelings is internal. They are my feelings, my reactions. They are caused in a stimulus-response manner on the unconscious or subconscious levels before rising into consciousness. The connection between the stimulus and the response may not even be known by the person having the reaction. A true morality for the human person cannot be built on such subjective criteria.

We might even say that the kinds of feelings we are speaking of are, in fact, an anti-conscience. The intensity of guilt feelings and their mysterious origins within our psyche tend to immobilize and paralyze our judgment and impede the development of a true conscience. Moreover, to the extent that our behavior and reflective judgment on it are dominated by avoidance of guilt feelings, we are also avoiding personal responsibility. The development of a truly human morality based on freedom and conscience can be arrested at quite primitive stages. In other words, we are prevented from ever growing up.

Humans are very rarely all one thing or another, but are rather mixtures of thoughts, feelings, freedoms, determinisms, judgments, and responses. Only the completely scrupulous person, for instance, can be considered to be totally immersed in guilt and utterly unable to escape from it. It is plain to see that the person who is guilty for everything is in effect guilty of nothing. Such scrupulosity, for all its anguish and inner pain, represents an extreme form of escape from responsibility.

REAL AND NEUROTIC GUILT

It is not possible to assess the goodness or badness of human behavior from the presence or absence of guilt feelings or their intensity. Conscience is a matter of reason and judgment combined with accurate self-knowledge and realistic self-evaluation. Conscience grows and develops as we gain maturity. We consciously internalize values and standards for ourselves as we grow. Many factors contribute to this growth of conscience. A rightly formed conscience evaluates circumstances, personal conditions such as freedom from internal or external coercion, and principles that have been assented to, in order to make a judgment on behavior. Values are understood to be relational. Rights and duties are appreciated within their context and reference to a world of persons and objects. There is also present a conviction that the good life requires attentiveness and discipline. These conditions of a right conscience contrast sharply with neurotic guilt which is essentially self-centered and self-absorbed.

The freedom required for acting out of conscience rather than automatically includes the ability to weigh alternatives, select options, judge what is the best course under the circumstances, and act decisively. Ultimately, the norm of behavior is love. Conscience demands that we act out of love. To be able to love consistently is the result of a life that is free, prayerful, and principled, rather than one based on whim, impulse, sheer feelings of the moment, or overwhelming passion.

Here a distinction must be made between loving others and meeting their expectations. If our decisions are based on trying to meet the expectations others have of us in the sense of trying always to please them, we lose our own grounding and put our conscience in someone else. Expectations are elusive things. Some types of expectations are useful, proper, and helpful, while others are very damaging. Social customs and rules of public conduct help life to flow smoothly. It is realistic that others should expect that I will live up to my publicly undertaken obligations. There are, for example, on the social behavior of a married man limitations which all expect and which flow from the fact that he has freely taken on the obligations of marriage. This kind of expectation by others is, in fact, an extension of an expectation that the man has for himself.

There are, however, other kinds of expectations that can cause us to act against our own perceived best interests. These are called manipulations. They are essentially an appeal to our guilt and intense desire to avoid it. One example of this is what I call control by the great TSK TSK. We might also call it the great scowl or frown. Our communities and families are full of this kind of controlling and dominating behavior. It is the spoken or implied criticism and judgment of our actions: "TSK, TSK, if you were a good religious you would . . . , or wouldn't . . . ." Extensions of the frowning condemnation are the silent treatment, the cold shoulder, the walking away in a huff, or the glare that kills. All are calculated to induce guilt in others for the purpose of influencing and changing their behavior. The most serious form of manipulation contains the threat of the withdrawal of affection or even attention. This threat is a very powerful leverage over another unless one is very sure of oneself and confident of his or her identity.

The expectations of others are personal obligations only when we freely assent to them. We can only assent when the expectation coincides with our own commitment. The congruence thus formed is based on someone's knowing my truth and relying on it. Then one can rightly say to me, "What you did seems out of character" or "You weren't yourself as I know you."

Much of what I have been saying applies to the whole area of authority. There is a legitimate authority that can command or demand certain behavior from me. However, as we grow, mature, and develop, we assume more personal authority. We tend less and less to grant to others power over ourselves. We are able to discern the legitimate sources and uses of authority as well as its limitations. We can exercise our choice to cooperate with authority; or if we judge it to be unjust, oppose it equally freely. Such an understanding of ourselves in relation to authority is far from mere rebelliousness or acting out against any external controls. Applying moral judgment to uses of authority represents, in fact, a high form of living by conscience. This point is illustrated by Fr. John J. McNeill, S. J.:

> Conscience within this perspective is a developing form of self-awareness; it is to be understood as the deepest self-consciousness of man insofar as it acts as a power of discrimination, deciding in every choice what will promote authentic selfhood and what will stand in its way. Man on

the moral level is characterized by self-development. He perceives every choice as a choice between authentic and inauthentic humanity. He sees his life as having a meaning only he can give it through his free choice. Moral obligations can only be accepted; they cannot be imposed. A psychologically mature adult can be called on to commit his freedom; he cannot be called on to submit it. For as long as a man is not directing his own activity on the moral level he is not to that extent a free agent. Consequently, to the degree that he is not a free agent, he is neither a responsible nor a moral person.[1]

THE GUILTY CONSCIENCE

Conscience most properly refers to the moral judgment that evaluates the rightness or wrongness of an action contemplated before it is carried out or performed. Conscience tells us ahead of time whether what we are thinking or planning is good or bad. However, what we commonly call a guilty conscience exists in us after we have done something we judge to be wrong. It occurs when we have acted unreasonably or have offended our own accepted internal values and standards. This awareness may or may not be accompanied by feelings of guilt. What is important here is that we must attend to the elements of judgment and self-evaluation independently of the feelings. We can be warned to undertake self-assessment by feelings of guilt, but the feelings themselves are not able to tell us about the morality of what we have done. In the event of our experiencing what is called guilty conscience, the way

---

1. John J. McNeill, S. J., "Freedom of Conscience in Theological Perspective," in *Conscience: Its Freedom and Limitations,* ed. Wm. C. Brier, S. J. (New York, Fordham University Press, 1971), p. 120.

to relieve it is through appropriate rational action. This action might include apology, restitution, contrition, possibly sacramental reconciliation, and resolution to change. Options are available to us in such circumstances to right the wrong, to restore the balance. If we ask forgiveness, there must also be present the capacity to receive forgiveness, what we commonly call forgiving ourselves. When this capacity is lacking, we are once again immersed in futile guilt feelings.

EYE TO I

True conscience is always in a dynamic process of development and refinement. In the context of this paper, it represents a continuing transition from the Eye to the I. As we gain more experience and freedom, our attention is concerned not merely with doing good and avoiding evil, but rather with doing the better, the holier, the more loving action. Our concern becomes more sensitively tuned to the requirements of relationships between ourselves and others and between ourselves and God. We can then utilize awareness of personal deficiencies and mistakes as challenges to grow rather than as sources of depression, self-hatred, and narcissistic remorse.

It is in this context that we can even view imperfections not as grave evils *per se,* but as a serious matter for me, since they represent the next steps that I can take in my own growth. They are welcome moments of grace instead of something to be avoided. These reminders from conscience do not paralyze the mature person, but rather are spurs to action and improvement. There is a healthy realism about all this which is a long way from morbid guilt feelings.

GUILT FEELINGS SUBVERT DEVELOPMENT OF CONSCIENCE

As I have said earlier in this paper, guilt feelings are anti-conscience. We all know of examples where relatively minor incidents caused intense pangs of guilt when more serious evils caused little or no guilt. There is the story of a Mafia don who killed with impunity and no remorse but wept copiously and with deep regret over forgetting his wife's birthday. There is no way a healthy conscience can develop in a life such as that.

Unfortunately, there is no escape from guilt feelings by simply willing it. Moreover, people tend to repeat the behavior that causes the guilt. Most of us have experienced such repetition compulsion, a feeling that we are in a rut, trapped in the same binds, going over the same ground again and again with no forward progress. The area of sexuality most readily lends itself to the experience of repeated guilt-laden behavior. Take, for example, the adolescent who "sins" in the area of sexuality. This "sinning" is usually accompanied by intense feelings of guilt, shame, remorse, fear. There is an equally intense desire to be relieved of the feelings. After the agony and torment of confession, there is often a euphoric feeling of relief. However, this feeling soon wears off and the pattern is repeated. This round of futility can be an extremely discouraging experience that stays with us all our lives. The confessional is not the appropriate forum for the relief of neurotic guilt feelings. In fact, confessors must be careful not to reinforce the neurotic by accepting or implying that the magnitude of the feelings is any true index of real culpability.

REINFORCEMENT OF GUILT

Let us now search ourselves for those incidents and occasions that feed our neurotic sense of guilt. Guilt-producing circumstances will be different for each of us because of all the factors that indeed make us different from one another. One common element is always a discrepancy in our awareness between our idealized self and our real self. Our personal "shoulds" and "oughts" come from an idealized self that does not exist and is impossible to attain here and now. When we live out of an idealized self, we are frequently caught in a double bind, an irreconcilable conflict of duties; and whichever choice we make will produce guilt. One instance of such double binding is what I call the "good religious" syndrome. The "good religious" is always happy, always available, always aware of God, etc. Yet as humans we can never be all of these things. In such circumstances, no choice can be right, no choice is free of guilt. I have known many people who have not received the gifts of the Holy Spirit as the charismatics experience them and are convinced with much guilt that they are resisting grace in some way unknown to them.

It seems that some part of us is always wondering what "they" will think of me. The "they" can refer to anyone: parents, children, peers, superiors, gas station attendants, waiters, or strangers nearby. What happens when I choose to take a nap or rest while someone else nearby is cleaning up? I wonder if Mary felt guilty listening to Jesus while Martha was doing the work. It is interesting that Mary did not (could not?) defend her idleness against Martha's guilt-promoting reproaches, but Jesus did. There are many kinds of events in our lives that can produce feelings of guilt. As noted, it is even possible to feel guilty over feeling guilty. Some people feel guilty about feeling good. When we are dealing with essentially irrational material, it can get very muddled indeed.

HANDLING GUILT FEELINGS

What then are we to do about guilt feelings when we have them? What can we do to get free of their tyranny? First of all, do not do anything. Dealing with guilt feelings is not a matter of doing but of awareness. Sit with the feelings and even try to befriend them. Once we find that we can tolerate the feelings, we are in position for some adventure. The next step is detective-like to trace where they are coming from. What event triggered them? What are the implied "oughts" and "shoulds"? Expose as much of the irrationality to the light as possible.

Above all, do not act out the guilt feelings to try impetuously to get rid of them. This useless activity is habit-forming and merely reinforces their hold on us behaviorally. Think of guilt feelings as temptations to abdicate our freedom and responsibility. If we can pinpoint those circumstances that cause us to feel guilty, we can resolve to deal with them differently. For instance, the next time a youth comes to the door to solicit for some cause, I can freely choose to support it or not based on the merits of the situation. This way we turn our feelings of guilt into signs pointing to our lack of personal freedom. We can then take them as a challenge to grow, to remove determinisms, and thus to become more human.

When guilt feelings are too strong to be handled by ourselves alone, we can talk them over with someone we trust. Sharing guilt tends to introduce objectivity and reduce the feelings to manageable intensity. Be advised, however, that the purpose in sharing guilt with someone is not to seek reassurance from them. It does little good to have someone else give us permission not to feel guilty. When we look to someone else to say to us, "It's O. K., don't worry about it," we are, in fact, looking for someone to give us pseudo-permission to be ourselves. It is an objective awareness that we are seeking, not facile absolution.

Finally, since guilt feelings are basically self-centered, our behavior should be such as to turn our attention outward. The center of our attention should be shifted from our internal feeling state to an interest in our neighbor and God. Almost every painful state can be alleviated by helping someone else and by prayer.

It is my hope that this paper will help to reduce the anxiety that is the result of thinking that each of us is the only one who suffers in this way. Guilt feelings are a common human experience. There is something grandiose in believing that no one can possibly understand what I am going through. We are all of the same clay, prey to the same weaknesses. In fact, this truth is at the very foundation of our system of faith in Jesus, who is our friend, redeemer, and savior. Were it not so, we would have no need of Him. Thus we know that God wants from us a service not of fear or guilt, but of love. As we are told in 1 John 4:18:

> In love there can be no fear
> but fear is driven out by perfect love:
> because to fear is to expect punishment,
> and anyone who is afraid is still imperfect in love.

Brother Sean D. Sammon, F.M.S., M.A., is a full-time psychotherapist at the House of Affirmation in Whitinsville, Massachusetts. A member of the Marist Brothers of the Schools since 1966, Brother Sammon received his undergraduate education at Marist College, Poughkeepsie, New York. He did graduate work in psychology at the New School for Social Research in New York City and is currently a candidate for a doctoral degree in clinical psychology at Fordham University. Before joining the staff of the House of Affirmation, Brother Sammon interned in clinical psychology at St. Barnabas Hospital, New York, the Franklin D. Roosevelt Veterans Administration Hospital, New York, and The Institute of Living in Hartford, Connecticut. He is an associate member of the American Psychological Association, the Scientific Research Society of North America, and Psychologists Interested in Religious Issues. His research interests include the adult development of American religious, and the fields of neuropsychology and alcoholism. In the past he served as a consultant for his province in the areas of formation and apostolate.

GROWING UP GUILTY IN AMERICA

Sean D. Sammon

INTRODUCTION

As the final curtain falls on Lillian Hellman's *Autumn Garden,* Crossman, a wounded and disillusioned midlifer, ruefully laments, "I've never liked liars—least of all those who lie to themselves." It is a bittersweet solace that he finds in Constance Tuckerman's response, "Most of us lie to ourselves, darling, most of us."[1] In part, these two former lovers, living on broken and empty dreams, are reflecting on a conspiracy in which adults have been involved for quite some time. The script of the conspiracy reads:

> A child is born. Within the first few weeks of life, exciting changes occur. There is physical growth, increasingly greater movement, and, in time, a budding

1. Lillian Hellman, *The Autumn Garden* (Boston: Little, Brown, and Company, 1951), p. 139.

"curiosity." With the passing of additional months, the child learns how to crawl; and eventually the child walks and starts to explore his/her world. There are dramatic and measurable perceptual changes. The child begins to talk and starts to develop some independence from his/her mother. Growth and development are at a gallop! Eventually, the child goes to school; and again we are struck by the significant changes which occur as he/she makes new friends outside of the family and neighborhood, forms relationships with teachers and institutions, and learns how to read, write, and spell. Development continues throughout childhood; and eventually, with puberty and the onset of adolescence, there is a tornado of change—physical, psychological, sexual, emotional, spiritual, intellectual, and relational. We refer to the adolescent as being "moody and changeable," in an "emotional turmoil," separating from the family, and ultimately going through a "rite of passage."

Late in adolescence, the first seeds of the conspiracy are sown. It is at this time that we begin to join in the falsehood and almost silently chant in unison that:

While there is significant, even dramatic, change for the first nineteen, twenty, twenty-one years of a person's life—somewhere about age twenty-one, this process slows and eventually comes to a halt. The curtain falls; and we have an adult—finished, unchangeable, and able to handle the challenges, tasks, surprises, and even difficulties of adulthood with relatively little, if any, modification of who he/she is or how he/she is in the world.

If an individual is so intemperate as to break the conspiratorial pact and admit that all is not settled, he/she is often tolerantly but firmly dismissed as going through "a second childhood," being in "middlescence," or trying to "work out something" which he/she failed to attend to earlier in life. The conventional wisdom argues that development does not occur in adulthood, or if it occasionally does, it is erratic and unpredictable.

Both you and I know that this view of development is simply not true. It is a fallacy to believe that while children change, adults only age. Our experience as adults informs us that even more dramatic changes take place AFTER age twenty or twenty-one than before and that the maps available to help us traverse the uncharted seas and landscapes of developmental change are very few indeed! Yet the conspiracy of silence continues.

Moreover, a trip to the local college library will give support to this conspiracy. Wander through the aisles housing the psychology books. There will be rows and rows, if not bookcase after bookcase, of texts and studies on childhood. The available amount of work on adolescence will be equally, if not more, impressive. However, the search for information on adulthood will be less fruitful. If much is found, it will probably have been written within the past few years and will be referred to as "groundbreaking," an "initial work," or will be restricted to a few personal accounts and biographies.

Fiction has always been a safe respite from the conspiracy. It has been permissible to follow such familiar characters as Saul Bellow's Moses Herzog or Eddie Anderson in Elia Kazan's novel *The Arrangement* as they struggle with themselves and developmental tasks in the middle years. We can even allow ourselves a wry smile as we identify with Herzog's opening commentary on his "midlife crisis,'': "If I am out of my mind, it's all right with me."[2]

---

2. Saul Bellow, *Herzog* (New York: Avon Books, 1964), p. 7.

But this is fiction, and we can again rejoin our fellow co-conspirators by pointing out how distant and separate it is from our own life. However, in all probability, our rush to devour the lives of such characters is rooted in our discovery of just how accurately their experience reflects our own. The tragedy is that adults do not talk often enough to one another about what is happening in their lives. The internal changes, the confusion, the dreams, the depressions, the excitment of living, and so much more are often left unshared.

I would like to begin this discussion by creating a frame of reference, i.e., a way of looking at adulthood. I would like to challenge the conventional wisdom about adult development by inspecting the various aspects of what it means to be an adult in America today. In undertaking our task, we may feel very much like the men described in the tale of the "Blind Men and the Elephant." The tale reads as follows:

Behind Ghor there was a city. All its inhabitants were blind. A king with his entourage arrived nearby; he brought his army and camped in the desert. He had a mighty elephant, which he used in attack and to increase the people's awe.

The populace became anxious to learn about the elephant, and some sightless from among this blind community ran like fools to find it. Since they did not know even the form or shape of the elephant, they groped sightlessly, gathering information by touching some part of it. Each thought that he knew something, because he could feel a part.

When they returned to their fellow-citizens, eager groups clustered around them, anxious, misguidedly, to learn the truth from those who were themselves astray. They asked about the form, the shape, of the elephant, and they listened to all they were told.

The man whose hand had reached the ear said: "It is a large rough thing, wide and broad, like a rug."

One who had felt the trunk said: "I have the real facts about it. It is like a straight and hollow pipe, awful and destructive."

One who had felt its feet and legs said: "It is mighty and firm, like a pillar."

Each had felt one part out of many. Each had perceived it wrongly.[3]

They had touched the trunk of the elephant but couldn't identify the animal, had touched the ear but were again unsuccessful in naming the creature. It is only after you have explored many different aspects of the elephant that you can confidently give it a name. The scope and difficulty of the task we are undertaking is to be able to name what it means to be an adult and to touch on many different aspects of the experience. The second focus of our discussion involves a journey. Using our developed common frame of reference about what it means to be an adult, we will examine just why it is that so many of us grow up guilty in this society and betray our dreams and the person that we potentially could be. Why is it that we come to the middle of our lives and find such a tremendous gap between who we have become and who we dreamed of becoming? Willie Loman is the middle-aged hero in American literature.[4] He is a tragic and broken man who fuels his life with empty illusions. By the end of this discussion, I would hope that we have been able to create a very different vision of the middle-aged hero and to answer

3. Idries Shah, *Tales of the Dervishes* (New York: E.P. Dutton, 1970), pp. 25-26.
4. Refer to Arthur Miller, *Death of a Salesman* (New York: The Viking Press, 1949).

quite positively that "yes, there are second acts in American life."

MEANING AND PURPOSE OF THE LIFE CYCLE

I have always preferred to look for the meaning in events and behavior. For example, in applying this preference to a person's emotional life, I consider it far healthier to search for the meaning of a person's anger rather than to encourage the individual to deny that anger or to push it out of his/her consciousness. Quite simply, it makes more sense to "make friends" with feelings, especially those that cause us discomfort, and to discover just what it is they tell us about ourselves and our world.

At the outset of this discussion of the life cycle, I would argue that the meaning of the life cycle appears to be a "journey inward," a call to come home to myself. The life cycle forces me to be more reflective about my life and its meaning. The more that I am able to be reflective about my life and its direction, the easier it will be to handle the changes and tasks which confront me throughout the course of my life. In addition, the developmental tasks which I am faced with at different points in my adult life foster a reflective stance and point me on the journey homeward toward myself. In theory, religious and priestly life should assist an individual to be more reflective and to examine the meaning of his/her life. It is tragic that in reality so many religious become "workaholics," and as a consequence are unable to allow themselves to develop a reflective stance toward their life. In the middle years, they pay a tremendous price for this inability, as does most of our society; and they experience depression, discouragement, and a feeling of being "burned out" and unappreciated. In honestly facing these feelings and searching for their meaning, midlifers often arrive at the reflective stance toward life which would have made the journey home to themselves much easier.

THE SEASONS OF THE LIFE CYCLE AND FACTORS SHAPING THEM

Nature tells us a great deal about the fabric of our life. The winter solstice, springtime, and the "dying days of summer" have, at different times, been used to characterize various aspects of a person's life. In the course of our lives, we pass through various seasons. Even a cursory examination of a few periods in your own life will bring to mind new beginnings filled with a sense of life and springtime excitement, as well as separations and leave-takings often marked by pain and a sense of autumn death. There are times when we are filled with a feeling of well-being and may imagine that we are in the summertime of life. On other occasions, we know only too well the bleakness and despair of our own New England winter.

As we journey through the seasons of our life, various forces and circumstances help to shape the structure of our life. We live in a specific socio-cultural world and belong to a particular race, ethnic group, socioeconomic class, religion, political system, and perhaps religious community and apostolic venture. We may have been born into a particular historical condition or event which has helped to shape the way in which we see the world and ourselves. For example, I am always impressed by people who grew up during the Depression era. That particular life event appears to have had a shaping influence in their life and on their world view.

We participate in our world through various roles. We might be a mother, a father, a religious sister, a citizen of a particular country, a priest, a friend, a lover, a religious brother, and so forth. We are members of different groups and organizations. Each of the circumstances that help to shape our lives and each of the roles which we assume during our lifetime allow us to live out various aspects of ourselves.

On the other hand, each of these influences and roles also inhibits certain aspects of our personality; and in choosing to live out a particular role, we must, of necessity, neglect certain aspects of the person that we are. This point is quite critical. No one life structure, i.e., no one way of being in the world, will allow me to live out all the various aspects of the person that I am. As a consequence, throughout life I will change my life structure in various ways in order to allow some of the neglected and inhibited parts of myself to be lived out. In periodically changing my way of being in the world, I find some factors difficult, almost impossible to change, while others are more detachable, more peripheral, and dispensable with greater ease. For example, religion and occupation, often felt to be central parts of a person's life structure, can be changed only with great effort and pain.

STABLE PERIODS AND PERIODS OF TRANSITION

The life structure of an individual does not change suddenly and unpredictably, nor does it remain static. Rather, it appears to evolve and to go through a series of stable periods which last six to eight years and a series of transitional periods which last in the neighborhood of four to five years.[5] A stable period has three critical aspects: (1) the individual makes certain critical choices about his/her life; (2) he/she begins to build a particular life structure around these choices; and (3) the person works to attain particular goals and values within this structure. For example, a young woman in her junior year of college decides to be a lawyer. This decision is a critical one; and in moving into a stable period, she will begin to build a life structure around this choice. As a consequence of the choice, she will apply to law schools which offer programs that meet her interests and needs. She will participate in any required testing and interviewing which would enhance her chances of admission. Hopefully, she will be accepted, complete law school, graduate, pass the bar exam, make professional contacts which will move her closer to her goal, and eventually begin practice. If the young woman's interest is tenant law, then she will have to build this value into her life structure. Another example would involve a young college age man who senses that he has a call to priesthood. This call involves a critical choice, and the young man builds a life structure around the decision by entering the seminary, studying theology, and advancing from ordination as a deacon to priesthood. He may have certain goals and values which he will attempt to build into his life structure of priestly ministry. Some changes may occur during a stable period, but the basic life structure remains stable.

A transitional period is one in which an individual terminates his/her existing life structure and works toward in-

---

5. Refer to Daniel J. Levinson, Charlotte N. Darrow, Edward B. Klein, Maria H. Levinson, and Braxton McKee, *Seasons of a Man's Life* (New York: Knopf, 1978), pp. 49-56.

itiating a new structure. Both the qualities of termination and initiation mark a transitional period. A person is called on to re-appraise what went before, to explore various possibilities for changes in himself/herself and in his/her world, and eventually to move toward making certain critical choices that will form the basis for a new life structure during the next stable period. Often a transitional period begins because an individual feels stagnant and complains that he/she is "in a rut."

It is important to note several factors here. First, a transitional period lasts for a number of years, four to five on the average. Change is not an overnight event! Second, a person must actively explore new ways of being in the world so that the critical choices which he/she makes in initiating a new life structure, at the onset of the next stable period, are not solely the end product of an intellectual exercise. A dramatic example of this active exploration can be found in the life of John R. Coleman, who was president of Haverford College. Coleman, spending a two-month sabbatical, worked as a sanitation collector, ditch digger, and a sandwich and salad man in a Boston restaurant. He did this unbeknownst to his faculty who, on his return, initially had some pointed questions about his sanity. It is interesting to note that Coleman worked as a laborer during a period when many people report a "midlife journey." In later discussing his decision and experience, Coleman remarked that he had often told Haverford students who had questions about their lives, the direction which they wanted them to take, and whether or not a college education should have a place in that journey that they should experience something very different from what they were familiar with, and that they should put themselves in circumstances which would throw their everyday existence into sharp relief. In this way, they might be better able to make the serious life decisions that they increasingly felt needed resolution.[6] Coleman took his own advice seriously and, I might add, was not sorry that he had done so! Our lives, then, appear to be subject to an evolving pattern of sequential stable periods and periods of transition.

THE ERAS OF THE LIFE CYCLE

The next important concept for consideration centers around the supposition that our lives are made up of a series of overlapping eras. As one is winding down, there are already signs that another is starting up. For the purpose of our discussion, the years of our adult life can be conveniently divided into "early adulthood," "middle adulthood," "late adulthood," and "late-late adult-hood."[7] Early adulthood defines the period from an individual's early twenties to midlife about the early forties. Beginning with midlife and continuing to about the time of retirement, i.e., age sixty-five in our society, we are in the period of middle adulthood. In many ways, this period can be our most productive and creative. Late adulthood follows this era and continues until late-late adulthood which gets underway about age eighty years.

---

6. Refer to John R. Coleman, *Blue Collar Journal: A College President's Sabbatical* (Philadelphia: J. B. Lippincott, 1974).

7. Refer to Levinson, pp. 18-39; and Wendy Ann Stewart, "A Psychosocial Study of the Formation of the Early Adult Life Structure in Women" (Ph.D. dissertation, Columbia University, 1977), pp. 5-10.

Indeed, the fundamental changing character of our life is what appears to move us from era to era. For example, a woman in her early forties may notice that she is reassessing the direction and meaning of her life, her commitments, relationships, and involvements. Her beginning sense that more years may have already been lived than lie ahead also dramatically influences the character of her life. Over the course of a relatively few years, she will begin to make changes and to move from early adulthood to middle adulthood.

When one examines each era more carefully, it is important to make some sharp distinctions:

1. In early adulthood (early twenties to midlife) there is a period which runs from the early twenties to the mid-thirties and which is viewed as a period of "novice adulthood." Those familiar with religious community formation programs will readily indentify with the concept of novice and novitiate. In a religious congregation, the novitiate is a period in which an individual is introduced to the life experience of the community, the charism which informs that experience, the traditions, customs, and history of the community, and the principles and practices of the ascetical and spiritual life which are integrally woven into the fabric of the community's life. At the end of the novitiate experience, candidates often report that they feel more like "full-fledged members" of the congregation. They experience less anxiety regarding their relationships with the community and find that their world and their life in the community are less unfamiliar and more predictable. The same can be said of the novice adult. He/she feels increasingly less anxious as he/she comes to the end of novice adulthood. The world is more predictable, and

they have learned what it means to be an adult. They have gone through a socialization process, have learned ways of relating to other men and women, feel more confident in their life work, and ultimately have reduced their sense of vulnerability.

Again, for a moment, examine your life about age thirty-five. You might find that, at this period, you began to feel less anxious that you were "impersonating" an adult, and increasingly more comfortable with yourself and in your world. There was an increasing sense of who you were and of the contributions that you were making to others, your community, parish, and relationships. You had by that time established some deep and sustaining friendships and felt more settled in the world.

As we examine the various seasons of many adult lives, we will find that there are similar patterns and that a certain amount of order is present in the development of adults. This finding is in sharp contradiction to the conventional wisdom that adults are stagnant developmentally, or erratic and unpredictable in any occasional change that they may undergo. In arguing for similar patterns and a certain amount of order in adult development, I do not wish to minimize the rich variability which is found in the life of adults. The following illustration may clarify this point. I have a good friend who is a weaver. Aside from the wells of patience which weavers seem to possess, one thing that fascinates me about weaving is the fact that using the same colors and type of yarn still enables you to get an endless variety of patterns in the fabric that you weave. The same seems to be true of adulthood. While many elements of adulthood, in terms of eras and periods, are held in common, the rich tapestry that each of us weaves with our life is unique and not reproducible.

In each era of our life, stable and transitional periods follow one another. For example, the early adult era begins about age seventeen or eighteen with what is called the early adult transition. Try to think for a moment about some of the things that eighteen year olds have on their mind. Among other things, they are frantically searching for ways to get out of the house. In our society, many young people leave home by going to college, entering the military, or beginning a first job so that they can earn enough money to move out on their own or to live together with friends outside of the home. Some seventeen or eighteen year olds enter a religious community or seminary at this point. Whatever the young person becomes involved with, the tasks of the transition period will make an impact on the decisions that he/she is making. For example, young persons who enter religious community during the early adult transition bring with them the developmental tasks of this period. In part, their motivation for entering may be rooted in these tasks. I am not trying to argue here for an "ideal" time in which to enter seminary or religious community. Rather, my purpose is to point out that the developmental tasks of any period influence the character of the decisions that an individual makes and the character of the life structure that he/she develops. This influence is true throughout the life cycle. The early adult transition appears to take four to five years and is followed by a period in which the young man or woman embarks on what is called the task of "entering the adult world."[8] During this stable period, the individual is called upon to

8. Refer to Levinson, pp. 72-84; and Stewart, pp. 97-99.

fashion a preliminary adult identity by making choices regarding occupation, relationships, and style of living which will define his/her place in the adult world.

In making these choices during his/her twenties, a young man or woman has two seemingly conflicting tasks. First, he/she needs to create a stable life, i.e., to "settle down and make something of his/her life," and to be responsible. Second, the young man or woman needs to explore his/her world and the possibilities that exist in it for adult living. They need to avoid making strong commitments so that eventually they will have from which to choose a maximal number of alternatives for adult living. Very few are able to achieve the delicate balance required for such a feat; and, as a result, some make early commitments, others do not commit themselves to anyone or anything, while still others commit themselves in certain aspects of their lives while choosing to "hang loose" in other areas. Any of these choices and directions have consequences; moreover, these consequences manifest themselves at the next transition period which is often referred to as the age thirty transition.[9]

The age thirty transition has been referred to as a "tremendous gift and burden." It gives the young man or woman a chance to make any necessary changes in the life structure that he/she has chosen for himself/herself. Often the age thirty transition begins with a vague sense of uneasiness and a feeling of depression. The individual feels that "all is not right." A person who committed himself/herself during the early adult transition may find that he/she is asking, "Did I commit myself too soon? Did

9. Levinson, pp. 84-102.

I explore enough? Did I know what I was getting into?''
The young man or woman who spent his/her twenties ex-
ploring the possibilities for adult living may wonder, "Do I
mean anything to anyone and what am I doing with my
life?'' He/she may feel that he/she does not have any roots
and will experience a considerable amount of pressure to
"settle down" and to make some commitments. The
change that occurs about age thirty is often more of a
"reform" than a "revolution." It is essential, however,
that during the years of the age thirty transition the flaws
and limitations of the early adult life structure come under
close scrutiny and that the young man or woman capitalize
on the chance for growth that this transitional period
provides.[10]

This scrutiny is especially important when we consider
the issue of guilt. During the early adult transition, a
young man or woman attempts to answer the question,
"What shall I do with my adult life?" This task continues
throughout "novice adulthood." The individual develops
a "dream" of how he/she will be in the adult world. This
"dream" or "guiding fiction" or myth which informs my
life may initially be a vague vision that is neither formed
carefully nor worked out. However, this dream must inform the decisions which the individual is making regarding his/her life structure. Some young men and women attempt to carve out a way of living the dream during the
entering the adult world period, and at age thirty they
evaluate their efforts and make any necessary modifica-
tions and changes in the life structure. They may also
rework the dream so that its spirit brings increasing vitality
to the life structure which they have built.

---

10. Ibid.

Others, however, during the entering the adult world period have fashioned a life structure which allows them to live out only a part of the dream, and these individuals may come to their late twenties and reach the age thirty transition with feelings of being increasingly stifled. For example, a man who had a dream of being a writer entered the business world during the entering the adult world period with the thought that he could write during his "spare time." His choice was due to family pressures experienced at the end of college to enter business as a profession; they were so great that he submitted to them and convinced himself that his family was right and that there would be enough time to write after he had finished his day's work. With the passage of time, he finds that he has little, if any, spare time once he has met his commitments to work and to his relationships with others. He may experience a growing feeling of resentment when work makes additional demands on his time. However, he is torn because answering these additional demands is important for advancement within the company. He feels trapped. The age thirty transition provides an opportunity for this man to address this tension. The decisions are not easy, and some losses may be entailed in moving his life more in line with his dream and in reshaping the dream to escape some of its adolescent tyranny. The age thirty transition truly is a tremendous gift but also a burden.

Still other men and women betray the dream and fashion a life structure that chokes any possibility of the dream's taking root and flourishing. Eddie Anderson was such a man. In describing this fictional character, Elia Kazan clearly outlines how Eddie missed the opportunities in the life cycle for change and for reorienting his life so that it was more consonant with his dream. In spite of this loss, Eddie Anderson's dream survived and returned with a fury during his midlife transition.[11] Later, I will discuss the dramatic steps which this man had to take in order to be true to his dream.

At age thirty, then, individuals may feel a twinge of guilt but may begin to see the discrepancy between who they are and who they imagined they would become. The meaning of the "vague sense of uneasiness" and the "depression" which the individuals might experience is clear. Both are a call to come home to themselves in order to make the necessary changes in the life structure and to rework their dream. This return to self is necessary because at the end of the age thirty transition the person must again commit himself/herself to a life structure which will serve him/her during the next stable period. These persons may find that they commit themselves to the same life structure which was theirs during their twenties or that they may be committing themselves to a new life structure. Even those who recommit themselves to what has gone before will, if they examine their life structure closely, find that the work of the transition period has affected the life structure. While externally it appears to be the same, in reality, it is somewhat different.

If the work of the transition period has been done well, the individuals will find that they advance within a fairly stable life structure during their thirties. However, if the work of the transition is flawed, they may find that they begin a long, slow decline within a stable life structure and feel increasingly hopeless or that they feel increasing

11. Refer to Elia Kazan, *The Arrangement* (New York: Stein, 1967).

pressure to break out and form a new life structure during their thirties. Both of the latter situations are painful and have implications for the midlife transition which begins about age forty. In some ways, those who advance within a stable life structure during their thirties are fortunate. This advance is a respite before the major tribulations of the midlife transition.

Finally, some men and women do not commit themselves to a stable life structure at the end of the age thirty transition. They find that they flounder during their thirties and that a sense of increasing despair is their lot.[12]

2. Middle adulthood begins with the midlife transition and continues until a person reaches his/her mid sixties. In our consideration of guilt, middle adulthood is of central concern.

Today, it is fashionable to have a "midlife crisis." Young men and women in their twenties and early thirties are reporting "midlife crises." However, in reality, it does not appear that a man or woman can have a midlife transition until at least his/her early forties for several reasons. Most importantly, the midlife transition brings with it a dramatic encounter with our own mortality, and this encounter makes all the difference.

The following quote casts some additional light on this matter:

> In the middle of the journey of my life, I came to myself within a dark wood where the straight way was lost. Ah, how hard it is to tell of that wood, savage and harsh and

---

12. Levinson, pp. 139-88; and Stewart, pp. 156-60.

dense. The thought of which renews my fear. So bitter is it
that death is hardly more.[13]

Dante wrote the above in the *Divine Comedy*. On occasion, the excerpt has been interpreted as an allegorical
description of the gates of hell. Others have argued that it
was truly a reflection of the poet's state of mind as he went
into exile and was far from his native city. More recently,
some commentators have rather flippantly suggested that
Dante was reflecting on his own midlife journey. Dante's
words reflect how high the stakes are at midlife. The experience is so dramatic and profound that "death is hardly
more."

The midlife transition serves as a bridge between early
and middle adulthood. During this transition, each of us
must come to terms with the past and prepare for the
future. As with all transitions, there is an aspect of termination and one of initiation.

Why then has the midlife transition drawn such considerable attention? Most importantly, during this period
we begin to experience incarnationally that we are going to
die. A man or woman begins to feel it in the marrow of
his/her bones. Several factors can be cited to explain this
phenomenon. First, until midlife there has always been a
"buffer generation" which protected us from considering
our own death in any but theoretical terms. Ahead of us
were always our parents and their generation, still alive and
active. In religious community, there were always the older
sisters and the older brothers. We could point out the older

---

13. Dante Alighieri, *The Divine Comedy*, trans. John Aitken
Carlyle (New York: Random House, Vintage Books, 1950),
p. 11.

priests in the diocese. With the passage of time and our entrance into midlife, we begin to shift generations. Many of us are surprised when we realize that we are no longer part of the "younger generation" but that rather the "younger generation" sees us as the "dominant generation." We also begin to take an increasingly parental role in terms of our parents. They depend on us for more support and assistance. Our parents may have died. The older brothers and sisters may also be dying; and in any event their number is probably diminishing, or they are becoming increasingly more dependent. The "buffer generation" is shrinking, and we are becoming the new "buffer generation." Second, some of our contemporaries may have died. When a young man or woman dies at age twenty-five, the death is eulogized as a "tragedy," and the life is characterized as having been "cut short." Many midlifers have given up reading the obituary columns in their local newspapers because they all too often find that someone their own age has died and that this event is not viewed as a "life cut short." Third, have you ever had the experience of waking up in the morning, walking into the bathroom, and looking in the mirror only to gasp in horror, "Oh, my God!"? The two pounds a year that you have been gaining for the last fifteen years have suddenly become thirty pounds of excess flesh. Your hair is a little thinner or grayer. Your eyes look a bit more sunken. Slight wrinkles peer out at you as though they were valleys in the Grand Canyon. You make a commitment to jog more, to drink and smoke less, and to lose weight.

In fact, all of these signs are telling you clearly that you are getting older and that you are going to die. The actual physical changes that you are experiencing may be, in reality, minor. However, from your midlife point of view, they are anything but minor.

Of course, we attempt to cope in many different ways: some of us deny the changes, while others of us believe that if we rearrange a few externals all will be well. The latter tactic is similar to the belief that rearranging the furniture in a room will somehow give us a new room. I am reminded of the comment of a recently divorced, middle-aged man who quipped, "Sometimes I fantasize about hopping on a jet to South America and starting a whole new life, but the trouble is that I know I'll be waiting for me when I get off the plane."[14]

Near the end of our thirties, we again feel the need to evaluate our life. A depression may signal this reevaluation. Again, it is important to understand the meaning of the depression if it occurs. We might find ourselves asking the questions: What have I done with my life up to this point and what have I done with myself? What are my greatest talents; how am I using them, and how am I wasting them? What do I truly want for myself and for others? What do I really give to and get from others? What have I done with my early dreams and what do I want to do with them now? Is it possible for me to live in a way that best combines my talents, my current desires, values, and aspirations? What I am suggesting is that during the midlife transition we question virtually every aspect of our life. Sometimes we are horrified at the findings!

Eddie Anderson is a character who has been mentioned several times during this discussion. His creator Elia Kazan

14. Nancy Mayer, *The Male Mid-Life Crisis* (New York: The Viking Press, 1971), p. 186.

relates that Eddie lost all touch with his Greek heritage even to the point of changing his name from Evangelah to Edwin and eventually to Eddie to satisfy the tempo and life-style of the California advertising firm of which he became an executive. Eddie Anderson also betrayed his dream of becoming a writer and instead became an advertising executive. Marrying a woman who fitted into the betrayal of his dream, he developed friends and a life pattern which almost choked his dream to death. The story of Eddie Anderson opens just after he has almost killed himself in a car "accident." Even he is unsure that it was an "accident." As his story unfolds, there is example after example of his betrayal of his dream. While he is sexually intimate with a number of women, he is, in reality, emotionally intimate with no one. His writing talents have been twisted into writing advertising copy and glibly smoothing the bruised egos of advertising clients. One day, he "packs it in," and predictably his contemporaries view him as being "out of his mind." His wife attempts to have him certified as "insane," and the family lawyer is sent to "talk some sense into him." The story of Eddie Anderson is really the tale of one man's attempt to return to the spirit of his "dream" and to rework it so that he is not tyrannized by the adolescent aspects of the dream, but rather revitalized by its life.

In addition to depression, guilt is a familiar friend of the midlifer. Guilt is neither more nor less attractive than any other human emotion. Guilt has its place in the entire array of our emotional life. It encourages us to "think hard" and check on our own morality balance. It is important that we do not run from guilt; it is equally important that we do not wallow in it. We have to let it do its job and then

allow it to move on like any other human emotion.[15] The
midlifer must deal with the disparity between what he/she
is and what he/she dreamed of becoming. If the midlifer
has failed to come to realize his/her most cherished
"dream," then he/she must begin to come to terms with
the failure and arrive at a new set of choices around which
to build his/her new life. If, on the other hand, an individual has met with some success regarding his/her early
dream, he/she must now at midlife consider the meaning
and value of his/her success.

Many of us, though, find that between what we hoped
to become and what we have become there is a gap which
now will never be bridged. There is a need for griefwork,
and we must mourn the person(s) that we will now never
become. We have to integrate better the tragic aspects of
life with the romantic view of life. With each choice that
we have made in life, we have, in reality, made many other
choices. With the realization that more time has passed in
our life than may lie ahead, we are faced with the fact that
we have taken a particular direction in our life and that
that "road taken" has precluded many others. A person
about age forty is not merely reacting to some external
situation; he/she is reappraising his/her life. What is the
fate of his/her youthful dreams? What are the possibilities
for change in the future?

At midlife, we begin in a serious way the process of
demythologizing ourselves. When we are young, we have
to believe that we are "larger than life" in order to do all
that is asked and expected of us. However, at midlife we

---

15. Donald Clark, *Living Gay* (Millbrae, CA: Celestial Press,
1979), p. 22.

must come to face our own poverty, our own limitations. We need to "deillusion"[16] ourselves as to who we are. There is a difference between "deillusion" and "disillusion." To deillusion is to recognize that some of the beliefs that we have had about ourselves and the workings of the world, beliefs that we may have held for a long time, are just simply not true. We are called on in midlife to reduce our illusions. On the other hand, to be disillusioned is a painful process in which a person is stripped of his/her cherished beliefs and values and is left feeling cynical and estranged. Feeling cheated, such persons demand that the world, others, and even themselves be the way that they imagined. Disillusioned people are hard to live with and will often ruefully remark, "If only I knew then what I know now." At times, in our exasperation, we might feel like telling them that if we had known then what it is they know now we would have most certainly told them, if only to make our life easier today.

When we work at deillusioning ourselves, we will experience a myriad of feelings. Disappointed, we will grieve and feel sadness; however, we will also experience freedom, wonder, and a sense of liberation. The experience will be similar to losing a friend or a loved one to death. The mourning will take time, but just as the relationship with someone we love is not ended by death, but merely changed, so also the relationship with ourselves will not be ended, but rather changed through the process of deillusionment.

Carl Jung saw midlife as the "noon of life" and argued that midlife gives us the second great chance to work on

---

16. Levinson, pp. 192-93.

the process of "individuation."[17] Individuation is the process by which a person becomes uniquely an individual. Jung comments that, in spite of the changes that we go through during our twenties and thirties, we are in reality not much different in our late thirties from who we were in our early twenties. With midlife, however, there is a chance to make more serious changes and chart new directions. Furthermore, working on the polarities that exist in each of us will expedite the process of individuation. Work on these polarities also allows us to deal more directly with some of our guilt. In this discussion I would like to deal with four polarities: young/old, creative/destructive, masculine/feminine, separate/belonging. Throughout the life cycle, at every stage of development there is a process in which opposite extremes are to some extent reconciled and integrated. However, midlife appears to give us a special opportunity to reconcile and to integrate.

To further clarify the discussion, I wish to introduce the term "archetype" which Jung uses to mean an elemental image, established over thousands of generations, that comes to exist in each person's mind. For example, in discussing the polarity of young/old, we may form a vision of what young means. For our discussion, the words "young" and "old" are not tied to specific age levels. An archetype gives us the potential for further development. The archetype evolves in a person from a rather undifferentiated idea into an increasingly complex internal image. Let us, for a moment, consider our image of God. In so doing, we will find that the image of God that we have

17. Carl Jung, *Modern Man in Search of a Soul,* trans. W. S. Dell and Cary F. Baynes (New York: Harcourt, Brace and World, Inc., 1933), pp. 95-115.

at this point in our life is exceedingly more complex and differentiated from the one that we had at age eight. We have had to work at developing the archetype. Archetypes either develop to a high degree or remain dormant. Jung felt that the process of becoming an individual is carried out, in part, through the work that is done in developing our archetypes.

To be more specific, I am going to examine the young/old polarity and the development that takes place in the archetype, "young" or "puer," and "old" or "senex," at midlife. When we use the words "young" and "old," we quickly find that our language is ambiguous. A fourteen year old boy may be found saying, "I'm getting too old for that sort of thing," when asked to join in a game with younger children. On the other hand, a septuagenarian may sagely state, "You're only as old as you feel," after having spontaneously joined in some activity with younger people. We use various symbols to characterize young and old. For example, the "New Year" is seen to represent youth, while the "grim reaper" is a figure which we more often associate with age. There are definite advantages and disadvantages to being young and old. To be young means to be "lively," "heroic," and "full of possibility." However, it also means to be "fragile," "impulsive," and "lacking in experience." Similarly, being old may mean that a person is "wise," "powerful," and "accomplished"; but it may mean that he/she is also "senile," "tyrannical," and "unconnected to life around him/her."[18] At midlife, each of us must find new ways to be young and old. We might have to give

---

18. Levinson, pp. 209-13.

up some of our former youthful qualities and mourn their passing. Others we will be more than happy to relinquish. The polarity of young/old is really what moves us from one developmental period to another. This polarity informs our experience when we are "in a rut" and stagnant. There is also a part of us which is forever being born and discovering fresh possibilities about ourselves. Because we in this culture fear the loss of youth, we have difficulty with the young/old polarity at midlife. At midlife, we have to accept the death of the youthful hero in ourselves and gradually discover which heroic qualities we are able to keep and what new ones we can develop. F. Scott Fitzgerald remarked, "Show me a hero and I will write you a tragedy." This declaration does not have to reflect the case of the midlifer. Willie Loman is not the archetype of the "middle-aged hero"; rather he is what our literature presents to us. Guilt-ridden Loman is living on empty dreams. Literature has always spoken eloquently about the journey of development, and most authors have written their most mature and profound works after passing through their own midlife transition. Having made the journey themselves, they appear better able to speak to what is most profound in each of us. The midlifer has to give up the mistaken notion that he/she will not be able to make the future any better than the past. Commitment to the tasks of the midlife transition, i.e., the honest pain of mourning and demythologizing ourselves, will make the future better than the past.

The creative/destructive polarity and its resolution have profound implications for the lifelong angers which each of us carries with us. Each of us has the power not only to be tremendously creative but also to hurt and destroy others intentionally and unintentionally. If we are to live at all, we have to accept the fact that we are going to hurt others and that others will hurt us. During the midlife transition, we must come to grips with this reality and with the grievances which we have against others for the perceived injustices that they have committed against us.

For example, if you are a religious superior, you may, at times, have to make decisions which will disappoint someone. A particular priest, sister, or brother may feel that he/she is more than qualified to be the principal of a particular school or the administrator of a particular parish or hospital. With your knowledge of the diocese or province, you might decide that this individual is not suited for the position that is open. When you make this decision, the individual who is turned down may experience a significant loss and may feel that he/she has been unjustly treated. However, he/she may not say anything about his/her feelings and instead bury them. The provincial has "hurt" someone. The hurt might be unintentional, but the person *is* hurt. The only alternatives are inaction or appointment of the individual because you do not want to hurt his/her feelings or make him/her angry with you. Both of the latter models of leadership are disastrous. If you are going to assume a position of leadership, you must come to grips with the destructive side of yourself. If you refuse to do so, you should not accept a leadership position because ultimately you will be a hindrance in the lives of many people.

The question now concerns the individual who was turned down for the administrative position in the school or hospital. Ideally, it would be helpful if that person could express disappointment and anger, and perhaps even the underlying feelings of rejection and fears of incompetence. This expression would provide an opportunity not only to begin the resolution of these feelings but also to allow others to help resolve these feelings. Sadly, because of mistaken notions about the place of anger in their lives, many religious and priests end up denying or repressing the feelings of anger and disappointment. The feelings, however, do not go away; they merely go underground. Have you ever had the experience of talking with individuals about an injustice that they perceived was done to them and have them relate it with such feeling and rage that you would avow that the situation happened a half hour ago? Only later you discover that the circumstances which were being discussed took place fifteen years ago and that half of the characters are dead. Yes, anger denied does not go away; it merely goes underground where it manifests itself as depression and guilt. At other times, it can display itself in a passive manner. Consider, for example, in community the sister, priest, or brother who always takes the car without ever signing it out even though you remind him/her at least twice a week that the oversight inconveniences everyone. They always have a good excuse, but sometimes you wonder if they are so doing to anger you or to craze you. They probably are, but also they probably do not realize that. Anger expressed "sideways" is not very satisfying for anyone. In summary, any work on the creative/destructive polarity demands that we confront our own ability to hurt and to be hurt and better integrate both into our personality.

The masculine/feminine polarity is one that has received considerable attention in recent years. Androgyny is a frequent topic of discussion. Masculine and feminine, as we are using them here, refer to the meaning of gender and not to that of biological gender. Male and female define biological gender. Each culture has its own gender images, and ours is no exception. Little boys are told that they are "not supposed to cry," while little girls are warned against being "tomboys." The indoctrination begins very early. In our society, there is a very sharp split along gender lines. The women's movement and the more nascent men's movement may eventually help to blur this division, but it would be foolhardy to insist that we have torn down the barriers just because we have begun to raise our consciousness. For example, when I was young and cigarette commercials were still permitted on TV, the Marlboro Man was a familiar character. He is another American hero, the cowboy who is a loner not needing anyone—a hard, tough image. We do have strange heroes in this society! Today, now that the Surgeon General has informed us that cigarette smoking is a health hazard and commercials for the same have been banned from TV, the Marlboro Man has been relegated to the pages of magazines. Even though today's Marlboro Man looks as though he shops in Bloomingdale's and has his hair cut by Vidal Sassoon, the image of the loner and that tough, hard exterior remain. Women are still often portrayed as dimwitted and seductive. The stereotypes have not changed a great deal. Hopefully, the future will bring the much needed dramatic changes that will allow us to be whole people, both masculine and feminine. In early adulthood, a young man often experiences the feminine side of himself as dangerous. A young woman may experience her masculine side as a threat. A woman may shrink from expressing her natural assertiveness and competence because she does not want to be thought of as too masculine. A man may suppress his more intuitive qualities because he fears their feminine implications. Another aspect which frightens many young people is their fear of their homosexual feelings. Rather than integrating these feelings into their personality and "making friends" with them, they view them as a dangerous aspect of the respective masculine or feminine side.

If a person carries the stereotype to an extreme, we have the inordinately responsible man who is experienced as cold and unloving, or the warm and loving woman who is characterized as an irresponsible scatterbrain. Men who are totally masculine are unable to be emotionally close to women because they view women as either maternal or sexual but not both. My own conviction is that each of us is not really capable of true intimacy until midlife. Each of us needs to come to know the masculine side of self and the feminine side of self. Many young men keep emotional distance from a woman because she reminds them only too well of the side of themselves that is feminine, i.e., tender, caring, nurturing. Along the same lines, many women keep emotional distance from men because to become emotionally close to a man is to come face to face with their own masculine side. Midlife gives us a special opportunity to bridge the gap between these two polarities and to develop them. Often, a woman can best help a man to come to know the more feminine side of himself, and a man can assist a woman in discovering her more masculine side. In order to so assist, we have to learn to make ourselves vulnerable to one another. Only in this way is intimacy possible. When I use the word "intimacy" here, I am not using it in the sense of genital intimacy. Some people have a great deal of genital intimacy but very little emotional intimacy. To be intimate with another person is to make yourself vulnerable enough that he/she will be able to come to know you as well as you know yourself. In each of us, there is always a part of us that remains unknown to others regardless of how intimate we are with another person. However, we can increase the possibilities for intimacy with others. As we come to accept the poles of masculine and feminine within ourselves, we are more capable of genuine intimacy. We are less threatened by others because we are less threatened by aspects of ourselves.

The separate/belonging polarity allows us to deal with the issue of solitude and the issue of belonging. Early in life it is important to be a member of the "tribe" and to be affirmed in that membership. With the passing years, it is also essential that we come into contact with our own solitude. There are aspects of ourselves that we will fail to discover and make friends with if we flee from solitude. Our fear is often rooted in the equation that society makes between solitude and loneliness. In moving toward increasing solitude, we become less attached. In midlife, it is important to find a better balance between the needs of the self and the needs of the society. A man or woman who attends to himself or herself and becomes less controlled by his/her ambitions and dependencies can be better involved with others and contribute to society in a more selfless manner. Midlife teaches us that ultimately to care deeply for others we must also care deeply for ourselves. This caring for ourselves does not concern itself with material possessions, but rather with human development and integrity.

The process of being an adult, then, is fraught with decisions and danger. We may betray our youthful dreams and arrive at midlife empty and guilty. However, it is almost as if life has a built in "failsafe" which does not let us, in the end, stray easily from our dreams. As we move through various stable and transitional periods, we are increasingly called home to ourselves and to what is most noble and genuine in each of us. The path of adult development mirrors spiritual development in many ways. In the spiritual life, we come to increasing knowledge and experience of ourselves and make ourselves vulnerable enough to God's Spirit so that God may take us on the spiritual adventure and ultimately bring us home to what is deep and genuine in each of us—God, Himself or Herself.

However, midlife is not an easy transition. We must come to grips with our own selfishness and stupidity; we must integrate the fact that love does not cure all ills and that life is very often unfair. We must learn to make friends with our guilt and accept the fact that we are in reality quite poor and limited but that, if we were not, we would be God. Man has always fled from being who he/she is; it is the original sin: man wanted to be God. Ultimately, midlife can leave us better integrated, more whole, and richer, more profound, lifegiving individuals. Helping with this task is the presence of "mentors"—those individuals who "mother and father" us and invite us to adulthood. They are a rare breed! Often the quality of an institution can be judged by the quality of the mentoring which takes place in it. After midlife, we are called on to be mentors to others who are on the journey behind us. Our work with them is our legacy, a legacy more lasting and vital than buildings of brick and stone.

James Baldwin, in reviewing Elia Kazan's novel *The Arrangement,* summed up the journey of adulthood and especially the issue of guilt at midlife. His poignant remarks remind each of us of the gap between who we have become at midlife and who we dreamed of becoming. They also offer us some solace about the journey of adulthood. In summary, Baldwin remarked:

Though we would like to live without regrets, and sometimes proudly insist that we do, this is not really possible—if only because we are mortal. When more time stretches behind me than before, some assessments, however reluctantly or incompletely, begin to be made. Between what I wished to become and what I have become there is a momentous gap, which now will never be closed. And this gap seems to operate as my final margin, my last chance for creation. Between myself as I am and myself as I see it, there is also a distance, even harder to gauge. Some of us are compelled, around the middle of our lives, to make a study of this baffling geography, less in the hope of conquering these distances than in the determination that the distance will not become any greater.[19]

---

19. Refer to James Baldwin's review of Elia Kazan's *The Arrangement,* in *New York Review of Books,* March 23, 1967, p. 17.

Sister Kathleen E. Kelley, S.N.D., M.Ed., is director of the House of Affirmation in Webster Groves, Missouri. A member of the Boston Province of the Sisters of Notre Dame de Namur, Sister Kelley received her undergraduate education at Emmanuel College in Boston and did graduate work in counseling at Boston College. Prior to joining the staff of the House of Affirmation, she served on the province administration team and held the position of personnel director.

LET TOMORROW TAKE CARE OF ITSELF (Matt. 6:34)

Kathleen E. Kelley

All of us—lay people, priests, brothers, and sisters—have a common bond. In a variety of ways, all are involved in the work of the Lord.

If we were to make a survey in terms of this common focus, the following profile might emerge: overwork, little leisure time; infrequent days off, not spent in preparing for work; a fair amount of pressure in life; probably a good long list of "shoulds"; some personal, unreached goals waiting "until there is time"; seriousness about life and often too much concern about one's responsibilities; a great deal of love, both waiting to be given and needing to be received. Probably the profile could be sprinkled with the guilt experience to complete it because the guilt experience is a part of our common bond.

In this chapter the focus is on several "hows" of guilt and worry: how we can let our lives be crowded and

87

pressured by worry and guilt; how we can walk down a road of life that is not our own because we followed somebody else's road signs rather than our own, for that would make us feel selfish and guilty; how, as people committed to loving, we can feel alienated through guilt and deprived within ourselves, despite our constant efforts to care; how we can avoid facing our growth as unique individuals by conforming to standards that others set for us; how, by not "letting tomorrow take care of itself," we can lose today.

That there are 1600 people present at a Guilt Symposium speaks volumes about guilt. Individuals probably attend either because they know nothing about guilt or because they have so much of it they want to find out how to get rid of it.

In fact, the experience of guilt runs through our lives. In life, many have closets full of experiences about which they feel guilty. Some things probably happened twenty years ago, but the experience is as real as if it happened this morning. These memories of guilts can haunt us. Often these guilty feelings focus on our past behavior: important things left unsaid, and then it became too late; the degree of care we gave someone or the way we felt we alienated a person, and now the person is gone; the wish we had, at age fourteen, that our beautiful older sister would fall down the stairs and mar her face, and then she did!

Then, there are the present guilts, those small daily twinges that we feel but often do not express, and that wear us down, waste our energies, and stop us from doing all we could do with our lives. This experience of guilt takes many forms:

the guilt of failing to respond to someone—or saying too much;

the guilt of taking a few moments for self when there are
so many needs before us;
the guilt of having three meals a day when so many are
starving;
the guilt of taking time for prayer when there is so much
work;
the guilt of working so much and missing prayer.

It seems that everything has guilt potential.

The reality is that guilt is a great motivator of our
behavior. We find ourselves doing things or saying things
not so much because we really want to, but because of that
voice within, the voice of guilt. That voice can motivate us
in two ways. First, guilt can move us to do or say things we
do not really want to do or say, but we feel the pressure
from others. Second, guilt can restrain us from taking risks
in life because of the pressures we feel from others or
ourselves.

An unavoidable part of our lives, guilt has many dimensions.

EXPERIENCES OF GUILT

What is this experience which is guilt? It can be considered as complex, pervasive, and subtle, yet potentially creative.

Guilt is a complex phenomenon because its sources and
levels are many. On the psychological level, guilt could be
understood as a signal system between our behavior and
our values. If I behave in a way that is consonant with my
value system, there is harmony. On the other hand, if I,
behaving in a way that violates a part of myself, act contrary to that value system, I feel the signal of guilt, experienced as psychological pain and often anxiety. This ex-

perience can be a very helpful one, *provided* our values are authentically Christian values which have been internalized. This situation is not always the case.

The earliest signals of guilt trace back to our beginning years. Since we were so dependent on our parents for existence, loss of their love meant death. Fearing disapproval and rejection from them, we learned to respond to their standards, "to be good," "to live up to their expectations," and "to take on their fears." Even when we moved out of the home, we moved their standards, their expectations, and their approval and disapproval with us. On the unconscious level, many people are still responding to life and still feeling guilty toward the parents living within them.

In addition, on a religious level, rules and regulations took a powerful hold on us, and breaking them in any small way meant the "fires of hell." These same rules, however, did help guilt to be more easily measured and worry to be more concrete. The rules defined our goodness. Our parameters were clear to us. There was safety in conformity. If one stepped outside of the boundaries, one felt in trouble and soon conformed to the expected image. A person was considered good if he/she did what was approved and accepted. Evil was assigned to the *nonconformist.*

In the past, there were different issues. I could worry that I was not perfect enough and could feel guilty if I closed my eyes to dirt in the corner. Guilt in this area had little to do with values betrayed and less to do with maturity of conscience.

Thus with no preparation for the rapid change that hit us, we were swept into the present. The present brought rules that are vague and parameters that are wide. Control is seemingly gone. Behavior now is not so easily regulated. We are not sure what to worry about so anxiety has become more free-floating. The questioning of values and standards in today's society is shaking the foundations that people have given their lives to guilt. The uncertainties of the present and future are causing people, in some instances, to cling to the past ways for stability, to hold back from risking, and to calm their anxieties in a new mode of conformity. In fact, conforming still remains the best protection against feeling guilty—conformity to others' expectations or conformity to others' inertia.

The demands of being human, of being religious, of being teacher or pastor are overwhelming. If our behavior flows from values and our values have not been internalized but still remain someone else's, we are apt to conform to their choices and their directions. The pressure for acceptance and approval is very alive within all of us, and the pressure takes the guise of conformity.

CONFORMITY AND GUILT

The culture in which we live promotes the image of being American in how we dress and in how we live. We are presented with the benefits of social acceptance, happiness, and security if we conform to this ideal image. Some people are filled with guilt for failing to live up to this image, the external demands placed on middle-class Americans.

Attempts are made to react to this pressure to conform through efforts at simplicity in life style and in communal sharing of goods. We try to stand with the truth that the externals of life are not important. But then to conform,

we often set up our own pressures that are much more subtle than the cultural ones. We make on one another our
own subtle demands and judgments regarding behavior,
involvements in ministry, and relationships. We expect
conformity to "the religious ideal" not so much in how a
person looks, but more in what a person is involved with
and does or does not do as a religious. And usually within
ourselves, we have parameters that define behavior, minis-
terial involvements, and relationships. If individuals conform to these expectations, we bestow on them the benefits
of social acceptance and approval. If they "deviate" from
our expectations and risk in areas that go beyond our
parameters of defining the "ideal religious," they can
easily be injected with the feelings communicated by our
verbal and, more often, non-verbal communications of
disapproval. The isolation and alienation that can be
experienced often force an individual to abandon any personal values and vision, and to conform, or to abandon the
church.

How often does one hear the remarks, "I don't fit," "I
don't belong," or "I can't identify with the group"? This
type of guilt has little to do with Christianity.

THE SUBTLENESS OF GUILT

As well as being complex, guilt is a pervasive and subtle
experience. It is a subjective experience triggered by either
internal events or external experiences. Guilt comes from
within ourselves as feelings: those private feelings of envy,
jealousy, resentment, or anger which stay hidden within as
guilt because we would rather not deal with them. We constantly compare ourselves; and when we do not measure
up, we feel guilty.

Guilt comes from without by demands made on us to respond. Others, aware of the power of guilt in their own lives, can raise these same feelings of guilt in us. We ultimately do what they want and give over the control of our own lives to someone else. Our resentment at being controlled produces more guilt. Rather than deal with the anger that comes from resentment, which also makes us guilty, we comply and pay a greater price—the price of losing our own direction and giving up our own personal choices. This payment is the subtlety of guilt. It can motivate us to respond in ways we do not want to; but we get so lost in the response we do not look at the source, the motivating reason for the behavior, guilt!

The response we make to others' demands can be masked in kindness, care, and concern. We can be praised for our altruism, our reaching out. The great hunger for approval within us all is fed by the praise we get for our response of care and concern; thus we lose touch with our motivation, guilt, and even with ourselves. We can reach outward not because of any internal commitment, but rather because of our guilt feeling. It was guilt, not our values, that motivated us.

Moreover, guilt can have us running in circles. I can feel guilty that I am not sufficiently involved in solving world problems. I become motivated to act, to be involved, but never to think why I am involved. This involvement may have little to do with what I really value. I can end up with a long list of activities but very little meaningful accomplishment. Conversely, I can be so dependent on the response from another that, even when I act out of my value system, I can still feel guilty. I can decide to do something good because I so wish. The response I get makes the decision seem bad. Guilt becomes unhealthy or neurotic when I feel guilty for appropriate behavior. I can feel guilty despite the fact that I chose to be involved in a good cause. We can spend so much energy responding to the outside demands that we never listen to our own needs. The result is that we layer our true selves with unfamiliarity, respond to the needs and values of others, and end up deadened to ourselves.

CREATIVE GUILT

There is a positive side to the experience of guilt. In our lives, it can be a creative force for repentance and conversion and changed behavior. If guilt, genuine or healthy, comes from a mature conscience, it will be that signal system between our values and behavior and that guide for moral human living. It will free us to grow in humanness and to grow in responsible adult choices. If guilt is genuine, there is an ability to distinguish between feelings of guilt and being guilty. If the experience of being guilty produces positive change in our lives, it does play a creative role.

This experience of healthy guilt has more to do with one's responsibility before God than with one's response to people. It has more to do with integrity and less to do with conformity. If I feel guilty at not having been myself but the copy of another, if I feel guilty at letting myself be paralyzed by fear, if I feel guilty at having blindly followed others instead of developing the unique gifts which God entrusted to me, if I feel guilty at being sterilized by conformity, and if I feel guilty at not living fully and loving fully, then I have had an experience of true guilt.

Guilt felt in this way is the special form of anxiety of life principles that have been violated and of reality that has been denied. Ultimately, this experience of guilt is the failure to risk being oneself. But this is a guilt we find hard to face so we let ourselves be overloaded with all the external guilts to help us avoid the real ones. Therefore, despite this creative and necessary part guilt can have in life, for most it remains a motivator of our behavior that blocks us from becoming our true, authentic selves.

AUTHENTICITY AND GUILT

We spend so much of our energies responding to others that the truth of who we are becomes lost.

Whenever I am not true to myself, my own feelings, my own values and convictions, when I skirt opposition and avoid necessary conflicts, or when I go along because it is easier, I face the guilt of betraying my integrity in favor of the guilt of conformity. But we do not deal with this level of guilt partially because we have not the time for such issues. We are too busy worrying, too anxious about too many things which block these issues from our attention and hence block truth. This condition brings me to worry, and it brings me to "letting tomorrow take care of itself."

WORRY AND GUILT

One of the frequent ways we avoid dealing with the issues of our true selves and attempt to handle the pressures of living is through the worry-guilt dynamic.

Worry is a very interesting activity. It gives us the opportunity to participate in everyone else's life, all major world issues, the economy, all crises, the ozone layer, and even the question of whether God is really doing His job. Used in a great variety of ways, worry often focuses on people, events, or aspects of self over which we have no control. It can be a great sapper of energy and an insulation against living fully in the present. Worry can be a real distraction that helps us avoid reality. It can be a self-indulgent activity that keeps our own private worlds rotating.

Usually, worry includes small things which prevent us from handling larger issues. Usually, it involves things that are not too likely to happen, and it usually focuses on the future. It can be read as concern for another, but more often it is a shield for guilt. My worry about a sick relative can shield the guilt that I have for not being present. A parent, worrying about a child's future, can mask guilt that he/she has not given all there was to give to the child.

Worry, defined as perpetual motion primarily in one's head, minimizes effective response to life and thwarts growth to wholeness. Worry becomes the perfect defense against effective action. "I don't have time to act; I'm too busy worrying." It can also become the motive for frantic involvement, usually leading nowhere. Defined either way, it is a powerful motivator of our behavior.

Worry, followed by guilt and then by worry, regulates our leisure, our work, our prayers, our relationships. It narrows our vision of life and provides a way to avoid the primary responsibility for coping with self and with one's use of personal freedom. We can easily worry today away, as well as worry life away.

REALITY AND GUILT

Today, the present moment, is a hard time to live. Reality has its rewards as well as its price. There is excitement in living today. There is a challenge to survive the pace, but this challenge can also be overwhelming. We all look for flight. There are innumerable pressures. From within and without, we are flooded with demands, all of which ask us to get involved. The media is not letting us "off the hook" but is facing us with critical issues—Cambodia, Iran, crime, hunger. This flood causes the guilt of our having too much of life's good things.

The impact of these realities is that they can become a source of guilt, a source of worry that we have too much in life and are not doing enough with what we have. But staying at the worry level will not move an individual to any answers. Becoming involved because of worry and guilt does not do justice to the effective development of the causes.

The result of these reality pressures can be that we, becoming over-involved and scattered, often collect causes and constantly respond to demands outside of us. The worry that keeps us in motion does little to change the reality or to enable us to face it.

CHRISTIANITY AND WORRY

The part of the Christian message that tells us: "Do not be anxious, do not be afraid, and do not worry," gets lost in the "busyness" of our living. We feel so responsible that we end up involved in all sorts of projects and campaigns; moreover, we lose our basic responsibility to be true to ourselves and from that trueness make choices for our involvement.

If our behavior flowed from personal values, our actions would have a focus, and part of that focus would be a realization of our limitations. We cannot be responsible for everyone or everything that happens; we cannot change anything by worrying. But the worry that runs around in our heads is a maze in which we get caught: a maze of trying to make sense out of confusion; a maze of a pace of life that is hectic; a maze of standards that are unclear; a maze of vague directions for the future. And underlying the worry of the future is the worry that began with us when we were children—the worry of acceptance and the worry of approval.

This worry is the one that shapes our behavior and involves us with people and in causes not primarily because of personal commitment, but because of guilt—the guilt of not being what we think others want us to be. Thus we give up being true to ourselves and conform to their expectations, conform to their unspoken judgments, and conform to their choices in ministry.

Yet the model we have for the non-conformist is the Lord, Himself. Perhaps we need to look at how He handled His responsibility of living amidst pressure, amidst change, and amidst people's demands. If we were to assess the way Jesus lived, according to the choices He made, we would probably fail Him. He was not always available. He was not always present. He was not always working. He had a focus that drove Him always to make choices to clarify for Himself the Father's will. He described Himself as "the Way, the Truth, the Life." He told us we should love our neighbor as ourselves—not instead of ourselves. He did not seem to think of what others thought of Him so He was able to be fully present to the reality. He said, "Don't be anxious or afraid, don't worry." He took time even when individuals made demands of Him. He went alone to pray despite the crowds. He socialized despite the needs. Of course, He was found guilty—guilty for the way

He lived. He was not the customary type of king. He did not meet the people's expectations. He was found guilty—guilty of being different, guilty of being Himself. He consistently responded to this call to be Himself.

There is no question that we can sit in a room of mirrors of self-development. We are called beyond ourselves to further justice. But justice begins as fidelity, the fidelity to the responsibilities of relationship to God, and to the courage to dare to be ourselves. Both bespeak fidelity:

to ourselves, to resist conformity, to assume the shaping of our own individuality through the choices we make, and to accept that we are human, limited yet graced;

to others, to respond out of genuine concern and commitment that flows into action—action that is effective because it comes not from worry and guilt, but from an individual conviction that the truth within demands such involvement.

Since guilt is the signal system between our values and behavior, it is in this area of relationships that it has largest scope, since relationships test our values and influence our behavior. Guilt can motivate us toward or away from God, ourselves, or others.

Try being a non-conformist as a response of fidelity to the Lord's call. Try being the only pastoral minister in a school community. Try being a poet or artist in a social justice group. Try working with the gay community in a suburban parish. Try taking a day off when the rest of the team is working. This non-conformity is the antidote for the worry-guilt way of living! Choose for yourself what no one else can choose for an individual. Choose to be yourself!

Vincent M. Bilotta III, Ph.D., is a full-time psychotherapist at the House of Affirmation in Whitinsville, Massachusetts, and is chairman of the department of formation ministry at the House. He did his undergraduate work in philosophy and psychology at the College of the Holy Cross, Worcester, and received his master's and doctoral degrees in clinical psychology from Duquesne University. Dr. Bilotta worked at Woodville and Dixmont State Hospitals in Pittsburgh, Pennsylvania, before he joined the United States Air Force. He interned at USAF Wilfred Hall Medical Center in San Antonio, Texas, and served as a staff member at Scott AFB Medical Center in Belleville, Illinois. Here his interests included working in the area of death and dying, training family practice physicians and residents in psychiatry, and dealing with individuals, families, and groups in psychotherapy. In 1976 he joined the staff of the House of Affirmation. He is a member of the editorial board of the *Journal of Fundamental Spirituality,* which recently published one of his articles. Dr. Bilotta has lectured extensively to clergy and religious across the country.

GUILTY: FOR BETRAYING WHO I AM

Vincent M. Bilotta III

My intention in this article is to share with you a perspective of making some sense of the experience of guilt in our everyday lives. My stance toward this human phenomenon called guilt is that it is a healthy experience. But in order to appreciate the life-giving nature of this experience, we need to slow down and allow ourselves space to dwell in our moments of guilt. My hope in this article is that we would be able to become more awakened to our sense of guilt, to experience it, to look at it and listen to it, and to understand its meaning.

Questions we may want to pose to our experience of guilt are: How do we deal with our guilt? What is our style of coping with guilt? What are the bodily signals that are triggered within us in the moment of guilt? How do we become more responsive to what our guilt is teaching us about our lives? How do we listen to our guilt as instruction for our lives?

In raising this issue of guilt for our reflection, I would pray that we would listen with compassion and gentleness. I am not inviting you to join with me in an exercise of blaming, judging, and punishing ourselves for not being perfect; but, rather, I am welcoming you into an atmosphere of becoming more mindful of our brokenness as vulnerable human beings.

THE EXPERIENCE AND FEELING OF GUILT

Let us begin by closing our eyes and quieting our busy minds and agitated bodies. For a few minutes, perhaps we could be still and recall guilt experiences from the past. Try to bring forth something about which you have had or still have guilt feelings. Place yourself in that situation and experience the feeling of guilt.

What does guilt feel like? When some people feel guilty, their bodies feel heavy and weighted down. It may be a restlessness, an edginess, an uneasiness, or an anxiety. There may be a tightness in the chest, upsetting of the stomach, a pounding in the head, or a heaviness in breathing. Our bodies may feel tight, rigid, unclean, frozen, numb, and low. We may feel small, exhausted, cloudy, and burdened.

Others describe feeling guilty as an atmosphere of powerlessness, of feeling caught, inferior, disliked, and rejected, or as a fear of being discovered and exposed. They feel abandoned, isolated, frustrated, and condemned. They feel caught in the eyes of others. There is a feeling of disapproval, a fear of punishment, a sense of failure.

REASONS FOR GUILT

While you are experiencing the many feelings of guilt, let me review some dimensions of human experience about which some may feel guilty. It is interesting to note that many people specialize in particular areas of being prone to guilt.

A person could feel guilty about gorging himself with food but not feel any guilt about ignoring the people at the dinner table. Some could feel guilty about masturbation but not about working eighteen hours a day. In what areas of guilt do you specialize? Why do you experience guilt feelings in one dimension of life and not in another?

One area in which guilt plays a major role in the lives of many is on the level of doing. Guilt emerges for being a workaholic or for not being enough of a workaholic. There is guilt for not measuring up, not doing enough, not achieving enough, and not being successful enough. Some people feel guilty for saying no, for setting limits, or for taking a stand. Others feel guilty for taking a day off, for resting, for not doing something every single minute of the day.

In the sexual dimension of life, some people feel guilty for having been born a male or a female. Some feel guilty for looking at their naked bodies, for touching themselves, and even for having a body. Others feel guilty about masturbation, sexual fantasies, homosexual feelings, or feelings of being atracted to someone; others, for looking twice at another person, or for having desires to be embraced by another.

Anger is another area in which many people find themselves feeling guilty. Some feel guilty for expressing anger; others feel guilty for not expressing their anger. Some feel guilty for not being "the nice guy," for making waves, or for asserting themselves. There is guilt for being angry at someone who is dominating, manipulative, and controlling. There is guilt for being angry that a superior treated one as a child. Some even feel guilty that they are angry when someone is taking them for granted, is using them, and denying their feelings.

Some feel guilty for the way they treat people around them. There is guilt for putting others down, for letting others down, for being late or neglectful, for hurting others' feelings, for not keeping a promise, for not being honest with others, and even for suppressing one's feelings.

Some feel guilty for who they are: for being an outlaw, for being a rebel, a renegade, a deviant, or for being someone different. Others are guilty for not being cool, calm, and collected; others are guilty for not being stoic.

Some religious feel guilty for thinking about leaving the religious life, for having loving feelings toward another, for feeling intimate with another, or for having a friend. Some feel guilty for living out a pretense of being a person of prayer. Others feel guilty for not being excited and highly motivated in their work. Many feel guilty for not being cheerful and happy all the time, for being burned out; many feel guilty for not giving themselves time for prayer and for not exercising fraternal charity.

On the other hand, many people do not feel guilty about not loving themselves, not being more flexible, not being good to themselves, not taking a vacation, or not resting when they are tired.

A PERSPECTIVE ON THE MEANING OF GUILT

The experience of guilt presupposes or is based on the belief that I should live in a certain way, act in a certain way, and feel a certain way. Guilt is experienced when I discover that I have violated the standard, the norm, of the certain way.

So, in guilt, there is an "I" who believes that there is a debt I owe to someone (whether that be myself or another) to behave in a certain way. If I fail to respond in that way, if I am not able to fulfill the what of that particular way, and I feel I am supposed to, then I find myself feeling guilty.

In the beginning, in childhood, significant others communicate to me a story of what life is about. They define reality and its meaning. They author and direct the script of that story.

Part of the script reads: if you want to be accepted, you will follow this certain script, this certain way of living out the story of reality. This is the story I am asked, invited, and sometimes told to believe. As a child I begin to believe that I owe to my parents or significant others the living out of this story. Another way of describing the what of the story is the rules, the duties, the governing principles of life. These are the standards, the ideals, the good, the order, the laws. In the story, I am informed of what I should do, ought to do, and must do to be a good boy or a good girl.

The others who define and tell the story that I am to follow in life may be my parents, teachers, peers, the priest, the culture, the television, or the newspaper. If I dare to become an adult, I may begin to assume responsibility to author my own story based on the wisdom of others.

Guilt emerges when I believe I should be living the story in a certain way, and I fail. Guilt is a violation of the story.

It may emerge as offending the story, as doing wrong, as transgressing, ignoring, resisting, or breaking the laws of the story.

UNHEALTHY GUILT

What would be the atmosphere of the emergence of unhealthy guilt? As I have described, in an experience of guilt, persons believe that they should be living the story in a certain way, and they fail. The more irrational, unbalanced, narrow, and unrealistic their perceptions are, the more controlled they become by the guilt feeling. The more dominated and determined by the feeling of guilt they are, the more enslaved by the tyranny of the guilt they feel, the more they are not at home with the feeling of guilt in their lives. The unhealthy dimension of guilt does not promote life. It does not assist in the unfolding of personhood. Rather, unhealthy guilt closes persons in upon themselves. It contributes to a self-consciousness that binds them in an atmosphere of being judged as bad.

Unhealthy guilt emerges within an atmosphere of the absolutizing, the totalizing, the onesidedness of the guilty moment. The more demanding people are of themselves in not being able to accept that they failed or were less than perfect in living a certain way, the more unhealthy the guilt feelings become. The more insecure persons are, the more ungrounded they are as authors of their own lives, the more they become ruled by the need to meet expectations and to avoid failure. Failure to these individuals means not achieving, not being successful, not being who they have to be to be accepted and affirmed. Within this atmosphere, to fail, to make a mistake, to be imperfect mean that a person's efforts are not enough, are not acceptable.

As an example of unhealthy guilt, let us look at the interpretation of Matthew. Scripture reads, "You must therefore be perfect just as your heavenly Father is perfect" (5:48).[1] A story is being told; script is being written. The significant other here is Jesus. Is the "must" rooted in the real or the ideal?[2] Am I going to demand tyrannically that I be perfect, whole, totally integral and harmonious with my relationship to myself and others when I know that I am imperfect, fragile, weak, on a journey toward integration and perfection, and that I will never arrive at being God? I know I really will never be perfect. But if I absolutely demand that I be perfect, if that is my story, I shall fail. In not achieving the ideal goal, the unreal goal, I will believe that I did not fulfill my rigid expectation or God's expectation, and therefore feel guilty in an unhealthy way. I feel guilty that I was unable to fulfill what was being demanded of me. Is the Father tyrannically demanding us to be perfect like Himself who is all love; or is He simply asking us to try, to struggle, to love?

The language of unhealthy guilt is one of harshness. It is demanding, abusive, criticizing, rejecting, finding fault with, accusing, blaming, condemning, reproaching, and scolding. It is one of impatience and chastisement. Persons are shocked and horrified that they made a mistake or are discovered as imperfect. They see themselves as worthless because they failed. Unhealthy guilt becomes bigger than life. It is seen as the beginning and the end. In unhealthy guilt, the image of the childhood story "Chicken Little"

1. Scripture quotes taken from *The Jeruasalem Bible,* Readers' Edition (Garden City, NY: Doubleday and Co., 1971).
2. Philomena Agudo, *Affirming the Human and the Holy* (Whitinsville, MA: Affirmation Books, 1979), pp. 19-24.

comes to mind. Guilt becomes the experience in which people feel that the sky is falling.

In unhealthy guilt, the judge, the author, the definer of the story of reality is external to the person. The meaning of the behavior is dictated and determined by the authority of the should. I rely on how the absolute authority interprets and judges how I should behave. I believe I have no freedom, no power to decide how I shall live this certain way.

HEALTHY GUILT

Healthy guilt is rooted in my assuming responsibility to become what I can be. The belief is that the certain way I should be is one of responding to author my own story. I am responsible for claiming the power for the authorship of my self. The standard, the what, the certain way is simply to be my real self. A healthy guilt would be experienced when I fail to assume the responsibility to answer the call of who I am by developing my true self. I am responsible to continue the creation of my original self. The failure to acknowledge my part in creation is not to assume responsibility for the gift given to me by God.

In Scripture, the parable of the talents (Matt. 25:14-30) speaks about a man's entrusting his property to others. He wants them to be faithful to what he gave to them and to respond according to their abilities. The reading seems to emphasize the responsibility of allowing my dormant self to emerge into its full humanness. My duty is to uncover my personal power and freedom and to grow as an independent, autonomous person. Healthy guilt would reveal itself in the failure to develop my true self and to hide behind the mask of a false, unreal self. I am gift. I am creation. Healthy guilt would be experiencing a sense of failure to assume accountability to foster the gift of creation that I am.

In healthy guilt I am the judge of what I have done and what I have failed to do. I am the informed citizen. I am the one who is called to define, to author, and to develop my trust in light of God's plan for me. I do not need permission from others to be my real self.

Powerful others will try to make me conform and live up to their expectations. I may have to run the risk of being defiant, of standing up to, and of going against powerful others. I am called to stand on my own two feet and to develop the ability to say yes or no in making decisions for the emergence of my life. To be seduced from following my path is to be controlled by others, to become a people pleaser,[3] and to be ruled by the tyrannical demands of others. Failure to stand up to others and to assume responsibility for the direction of my life and the promotion of love in light of God's design for me should engender healthy guilt.

The feeling of guilt that emerges from a healthy individual is rooted in the belief that the task of each of us is to decipher what my story is, what the meaning of my life is, and what the hierarchy of values that guide my life is. Healthy guilt reveals itself within a perspective that perceives a sense of failure not as the end of the world but as an encounter with my personal humanity. My violation or failure is seen in light of the horizon that I am called by

3. Joseph L. Hart, "Perils of the Pleaser" in *Loneliness: Issues of Emotional Living in an Age of Stress for Clergy and Religious,* ed. James P. Madden, C.S.C. (Whitinsville, MA: Affirmation Books, 1977), pp. 41-55.

God to do and to be my best. The Lord is asking me only to try to be who I am. He is not asking me to arrive at total personal integration or complete personal development.

Here, it is important to be reminded that it is in the struggle of trying to respond to who I am that my sanctity resides. I can only struggle to be who I am. In assuming responsibility to discover what it means to be human, I realize in a deeper way that integration is not something that I arrive at but it is something that I struggle to maintain.

BETRAYAL OF THE BODY[4]

To hand over the responsibility of the authorship of my life to another is to betray who I am called to be. Thomas Merton, in his book *New Seeds of Contemplation,*[5] speaks of the call to sanctity as the finding out of who I am, discovering my true self, and being my self.

I would like to take up the issue of responsibility of fostering my true self by focusing in on the guilt of betraying my body. I am called to discover, own, live in, and befriend my body. I need to remain faithful to the fact that my body and its senses ground me in reality. I experience and know the reality of creation and God through my body and its senses.

St. Bonaventure, in his work *The Mind's Road to God,*[6] points out that God enters our lives through the doors of

---

4. Refer to Alexander Lowen, *The Betrayal of the Body* (New York: Collier Books, 1969).
5. Thomas Merton, *New Seeds of Contemplation* (New York: New Directions, 1972), p. 31.
6. St. Bonaventure, *The Mind's Road to God* (New York: Bobbs-Merrill, 1953), p. 14.

our five senses. God is revealed not only through sensible things but in them. The tracings of the Lord proclaim His presence. Our bodies become the vehicle for God to reach out to us. Through our bodies the Lord imperceptibly stirs within us a desire to be in union with Him. St. Bonaventure implies that, through the dialogue between our body senses and the tracings of God in the sensible signs of everyday life, God's inaccessibility is made accessible to us. In and through our bodily interactions with the world around us, the presence of God reaches us.

Healthy guilt emerges when we recognize that we have betrayed the responsibility of being who we are by betraying our bodies. We were all given a body at birth; but many parents took our bodies back by not allowing us to live in them, by relating the story that our bodies are evil and a temptation to sin. For some of us, the body was reduced to an it, and treated as a thing, a tool, a functional object. The author of the story that our bodies are corrupt invited people to turn against their bodies as dangerous enemies and to avoid their bodies by not paying attention to them.

Many people have been asked to trade in their bodies and to make believe that they do not have one. For years, people have been encouraged not to accept or identify with their bodies, to do little with them, and to be at war with them. Their bodies have been strangers to them and something of which they are ashamed.

This process of forsaking their bodies, giving up on, and abandoning their bodies is the process of the betrayal of the body, and thus a disowning of the real self. People who betray their bodies should feel guilty for not responding to their original selves.

But even if you were not a victim of this implicit brain-washing process of betraying your body, how can you betray your body now? We may be betraying our bodies by not taking care of them, by mistreating them, by not listening to, or by not befriending them.

Some examples of abusing myself and my body would be obesity, overeating, eating junk food, pushing myself to exhaustion, not taking time for my body's physical needs, not getting proper physical exercise, and allowing tension and stress to riddle my body. Others may be involved in self-abuse when they betray the affective dimension of their lives by ignoring their feeling, hiding their feelings, not having the courage to discover their feelings or to own them, swallowing anger, and holding back tears that need to be released.

The process of betraying my body and becoming immersed in my head emerges gradually in the flow of the everyday. Day in and day out, the world seems to rush in on me and calls me forth out of my body. The television, the newspapers, the radio, the billboards on the highways, all seem to be competing for my attention. My mind becomes overstimulated. The rational, the logical, the analytical seem to take over my life. The world rushes in on me. It grabs me, chokes me, and overtakes me. The "hecticness" of my everyday life seems to claim my body. The noise, the traffic, the tension, and the speed pull me out of my body.

The betrayal of the body is lived out more concretely in the experience of being in my head. People who are living in their heads may be described as daydreamers, off in another world, up in the air, having their heads in the clouds, not having their feet on the ground, out of touch, not in tune, out of it, heady, and abstract. These people may also be described as spaced out, not accessible, floating away, fogged up, withdrawn, distant, unavailable, out of it, and not there.

In the book *Zorba the Greek,* by Nikos Kazantzakis, the character named Boss describes this abandonment well when he says:

> My life has gone on the wrong track, and my contract with men has now become a mere soliloquy. I had fallen so low that, if I had to choose between falling in love with a woman and reading a book about love, I should have chosen the book.[7]

Again in *Zorba the Greek,* Zorba, speaking to the Boss, says:

> What are you thinking about? You keep a pair of scales, too, do you? You weigh everything to the nearest gram, don't you? Come on, friend, make up your mind. Take the plunge![8]

You may have met the little boy who discovered that he was not acceptable to his peers in the sports arena because he lacked physical coordination so he took flight into his head by becoming the intellectual of the class.

Other examples of being in your head would be your driving along a highway and almost hitting another car because you were in your head and not paying total attention to the bodily activity of driving safely. Many people eat their food but never taste it because their minds are busy about other, more important matters.

Imagine yourself trying to pick up pieces of glass when you are in your head and not paying attention to what you

7. Nikos Kazantzakis, *Zorba the Greek* (New York: Simon and Shuster, Inc., 1952), p. 101.
8. Ibid., p. 10.

are doing. Or you could be walking up a flight of stairs; and because you are not living in your feet, you trip and fall. Imagine trying to drive in a snowstorm on slippery icy roads, and your mind is somewhere else. Once your body loses touch with the road because you no longer have a feel for the road as you are driving along, the car will probably begin to spin around, and you will lose control of the wheel.

I remember the trouble I got myself into when I was about ten years old, and I was just walking around in my head. It was a Thursday evening during the summer. My mother had dropped me off downtown to do a few errands for her. As I was walking along the sidewalk, I noticed a parade going by. It was the women in the local town beauty pageant. I got so caught up in looking at these attractive women that I crashed into a parking meter as I was walking along. Blood began to cover my face. The reality of not paying attention to where I was going spoke loudly and clearly to me. How would I explain the gash on my forehead to my mother? How could I tell her that I was fantasizing about these women and that I became out of touch with the reality of doing her errands?

Many people betray their bodies by getting lost in their private, inner selves. Their minds become filled with the noise of figuring, analyzing, and calculating the world and people around them. Their heads are buzzing with a jumble of words, ideas, and questions. They become observers of themselves, spectators of life, and not livers of it. These introspective persons seem to use up their psychic energy in trying to control what is around them.

When I was in the Air Force and stationed at a command headquarters, I became familiar with the command post, where people are on top of everything that is going on in their command. This particular command was in charge of the world airlift. With a large map of the world facing them, all day and all night, men would plot out the exact location of every single airplane that was part of their airlift command.

People who are walled up within their own little world ot their private selves are living behind their head in their own particular command post. Their mind is like a radar set that scans the outer reality before them. The outer reality has to be constantly watched, constantly controlled. The command post, the control tower, must always be on ready alert to defend itself in case of attack. So there we are, hidden in our command post and vigilantly guarding ourselves from being seen as we are. Locked up in our heads, we become withdrawn from the flow of daily life so that we can be in constant charge and control of what others are able to see of who we are. We must always protect ourselves from being seen as we really are. We are afraid to let people enter our lives. No one is allowed to see our imperfect selves.

I am ashamed of the limited person I am. People will definitely reject me if they see how impoverished I really am. In my command post, I become lost in the dark recesses of worrying about what people think of me. I am anxious that they will discover my fragile humanity. I am afraid that my imperfect real self will be exposed; then I shall be rejected as not good enough.

This style of living in my head, living behind my head in my command post, fosters a split from being present to the greater whole of reality. The command post experience is very narrowing and limiting. While I am in my command post stance, I am unable to be in my body and to be open through the senses of my body to all that is around. It is like seeing and experiencing life from a peep hole. I can experience only what is directly in front of me. In my command post, I am so busy vigilantly protecting myself that I get lost in my head as I watch the radar set and build barriers that will prevent my real self from being exposed.

THE BETRAYAL OF THE SPIRITUAL LIFE

As I have already stated, we are responsible to ourselves, others, and God to become who we are. To answer the call of who we are is to develop the gift of creation that we are. Hopefully, we can grow into a sense of guilt when we find ourselves failing to respond to the gift of the vulnerable self that we are.

We are called to be a whole self, not a fragmented self. To betray the bodily dimension of our existence is to betray who I am. The abandoning of the body is also the abandonment of the development of a rich, spiritual life. If I do not live in my body, I am unable to become awakened to the nearness of God around me.

Merton speaks about the importance of the body in the spiritual life when he says, "We all [our bodies] become doors and windows through which God shines back into His own House."[9] In St. Paul, we hear: "Your body, you know, is the temple of the Holy Spirit, who is in you since you received Him from God" (1 Cor. 6:19). To be in touch with my body is to become awakened to the fact that God is residing within me. The abode of God is within me. It is through our bodies that we discover God. It is through our

9. Merton, p. 67.

bodies that we come in touch with God as He reveals Himself to us from within and without. It is through our bodies that we extend the love of God to others. It is through our bodies that we love God.

The certain way that we are being asked to respond to ourselves is to be open to our original selves. The core of our original selves is the spiritual dimension of our existence. Many of us today can easily develop a style in which we betray the spiritual dimension of our existence. In failing to respond to this central dimension of our existence, we may find ourselves experiencing a feeling of guilt. Feeling guilty for the abandonment of our spiritual development presupposes that we believe that the unfolding of our spiritual life is most important for the emergence of our gift as a human person. Many agree in principle that the spiritual dimension of our personalities is important, but in practice we tend to betray this response to who we are as we betray our bodies. For many people, the level of consciousness of guilt for betraying the responsibility to become the spiritual person we are called to be is non-existent.

The prophet Jeremiah in the Old Testament addresses himself to this issue when he speaks about the need to make a new covenant. In his writings, Jeremiah points out that people had become preoccupied with objectively performing all the legal, ritual requirements and regulations of the covenant. The people's ability to respond to Yahweh was that of not violating the external, the outward fulfillment of the law. These people betrayed the spiritual dimension of their existence. Jeremiah describes Israel of the Old Testament as smug, overconfident, complacent, obstinate, and lost in a false security of their own power and egoism. Their hearts became insensible, calloused, empty, heavy, hardened, and rebellious. This hardness of heart led to a theoretical head knowledge of God. The Israelites at the time of Jeremiah became specialists in the law and theological abstractions but not in experiencing the nearness of God in their everyday lives.

As we know from Old Testament theology, the heart was the expression of the spiritual in man.[10] The heart was the element of responsibility. Jeremiah informs us that, in order for Yahweh's people to know Him, the hard scale which grew over their hearts must be removed (31:33). The hardness of Israel's heart must be broken in order for God's people to come back to Him. The interior dimension of Israel's being must be uncovered and made ready again to encounter the Lord.

From Jeremiah, we discover that to respond to my true self, my whole self, I must cultivate my interior life (31:33). This cultivation requires that I soften my heart, give up being stubborn, and develop a purity of heart, a single-mindedness that gives my attention to the nearness of God. A change of heart would be rooted in an openness of my body to the tracings of God in all that is around me.

OBSTACLES TO THE AWARENESS OF GUILT

For many people, the experience of being guilty for betraying their bodies and their interior lives is not something that is part of their everyday lives. The hectic style of the everyday becomes an obstacle to people's being able to tune into an awareness of the feeling of guilt. The image that comes to mind is one of a DC-10. Many of us

---

10. Refer to Walter Eichrodt, *Theology of the Old Testament,* trans. S. A. Baker, vol. 2 (Philadelphia: Westminster, 1967).

tend to be flying around at a speed of four hundred miles an hour and a height of 39,000 feet. This, indeed, is living in my head. Traveling in my everyday life at this speed and this altitude, I cannot help being out of touch with what is occurring on the ground and inside me on a feeling level. Moving too fast and being in the clouds become obstacles to being aware of any guilt feelings in my life. Under these circumstances, I cannot hear the voice of guilt because I have successfully silenced it.

In flying so high and so fast, I become out of touch with my responsibilities. I am no longer able to respond to what is on the ground. While seated in the cabin of a DC-10, I am in my own little world above the clouds. I may be flying high in striving for success, in striving to be approved by others, and in avoiding failure and insecurity. My body is no longer rooted in the earth. I am ungrounded and disembodied. The DC-10 experience is being split from the everyday reality of my life. While I am in my DC-10, the reality that is going on below me is unable to inform me as to what is going on. The DC-10 experience is a protection from hearing, seeing, and tasting the world below. I am not aware of what is happening on the ground. I am drifting along on top of the world. From this safe perspective of 39,000 feet, I cannot feel what is happening below. I am living in my head, living from the neck up; and, as a result, I am unable to feel guilty about anything because I do not feel anything. I am no longer connected to the real world. In flight at four hundred miles an hour and 39,000 feet off the ground, I am able to evade and to escape what is happening on the ground in my real world.

Other images of obstacles to feeling guilt are a refrigerator or an air conditioner. If you have ever listened and paid attention to a refrigerator or air conditioner, you perhaps will discover that it hums. There are no ups or downs but a persistent monotone of humming. Hum! Hum! The senses are dimmed and lulled to sleep.

An obstacle to the experience of guilt is one's becoming a hummer. I begin to live my life as a hummer: no ups, no downs . . . complacently there . . . just humming a monotone. And there I am: unable to feel, to sense, and to flow with what is around. I am unable to respond to the how of living my life. As a hummer, I am just there: not awake, not aware, just numb from the humming.

As a hummer, I have abandoned my ability to tune in and respond to what is around me. As a hummer, I abuse myself. I violate my call to wholeness and intouchness. As a hummer living in my head, I betray the actualizing of the gift of my unique humanity. My real self is buried and remains dormant. Humming is a one-sided accent on reality. A process of forsaking my body, it becomes an obstacle to the awareness of guilt in my life.

GUILT AS A GUIDE FOR MY LIFE

Guilt is an important guide for my life. If I give myself space to listen to this feeling, it may become an opportunity to understand myself. Guilt can be a helpful teacher for me if I am willing to struggle to allow it to reveal its meaning to me and to learn from this meaning.

The experience of guilt can be an invitation to stop, look, and listen to who I am and what I am up to in my life. It can keep me honest with how I am living my everyday life. As a friend, guilt may raise the question of how I have been treating myself and others. How have I been responding to myself and others as gifts, as God's creation?[11] How have I been promoting what has been entrusted to me by the Creator?

Moreover, the inner stirrings of guilt could remind me that I am betraying the body that I am. Guilt may reveal that I am not being present to others in the here and now because I have abandoned my senses and am specializing in living in my head. The experience of guilt may be speaking about the fact that I have been totally lost in the value of doing by being absorbed in the immediate practical, the superficial, and the mere functional. The restlessness of my body in the experience of guilt may be proclaiming that I have been split from the spiritual dimension of life where I am open to wonder, mystery, the simple, and the sacred. My deeper, interior self may have been covered over by my feverish activity of proving that I am acceptable and, in the process, forsaking my body and the vital dimension of my existence.

The experience of guilt may also bring me back to the process of remembering who I am. Guilt may be an opportunity to rediscover that I am still trying to be someone I am not. Through the experience of guilt, I may become more open to how I am trying to live out a false, idealized self.

In *Zorba the Greek,* Zorba tells the story of what happened to a crow who tried to live out a false self:

> Well, you see, this crow used to walk respectably, properly—well, like a crow. But one day he got it into his head to try to strut about like a pigeon. And from that time on the poor fellow couldn't for the life of him

---

11. Refer to Thomas A. Kane, *The Healing Touch of Affirmation* (Whitinsville, MA: Affirmation Books, 1976).

recall his own way of walking. He was all mixed up, don't you see? He just hobbled about.[12]

The feeling of guilt presents the opportunity of reuniting with my true, original self. It provides me with the occasion to reconcile my ideal self with my real self. When I live my life from the perspective of unrealistic standards controlling my life, I am not responding to the reality of who I am. I may feel guilty because I am always losing, I am never perfect, never complete, never quite living in the manner in which I am supposed to be living.

In guilt, I may discover that I have betrayed who I am. The experience of listening to my guilt may open up an access to realize that I do not have to be shocked that I am an imperfect and limited human being. The "real me" is impoverished and incomplete. Guilt can be an invitation to respond to the "real me." It can be a call to be an advocate of the "real me."

What is the certain way of the "real me"? The "real me" is evolving. The who I am evolves over time. This growth over time is gradual. In order to develop a respect for the process of the growth of who I am, I need to develop an eye for the gradual. Change is gradual. There is a gradualness to the unfolding of the real.

For example, I remember planting my garden last spring. The instructions on the back of the seed package stated that the vegetables would mature in about sixty-eight days. After I had planted the seeds one evening, the next morning I was in the garden to discover what growth had taken place during the night. The child in me was disappointed. I had not surrendered to the way of the gradual. I did not surrender to the real.

---

12. Kazantzakis, p. 67.

Thus I may find myself prone to guilt because I am not devoted to reality. I may not be devoted to the process of the gradual. I need to grow into what St. Francis de Sales describes as the *Devout Life.*[13] I need to approach myself from the perspective of the values of the spiritual life. These values are rooted in love, patience, compassion, and gentleness toward myself and others. I need to give myself space and time to grow with the gradual unfolding of my reality.

If I befriend my guilt experiences, perhaps they will guide me along my path to God. Guilt may be a gentle, silent whispering that I am in the process of betraying who I am. If I am aware of this moment of betrayal, then I have another opportunity to remember who I am.

I am gift, and I am called to try to unfold the process of my creation and that of the world around me. I am called to struggle to grow in and with the nearness of God around me and within me.

---

13. Refer to St. Francis de Sales, *Introduction to the Devout Life,* trans. John K. Ryan (Garden City, NY: Doubleday and Co., 1966).

Reverend Joseph L. Hart, S.S.E., Ph.D., is director of the House of Affirmation, Whitinsville, Massachusetts. He has been associated with the House for several years, and served for six months as consultant to Heronbrook House in England when this affiliate of the House of Affirmation first opened. A priest of the Society of St. Edmund, ordained in 1955, Father Hart studied theology at St. Edmund's Seminary. He received his doctorate at the Catholic University of America and did post-doctoral study at the Alfred Adler Institute in Chicago. He is a member of the North American Society of Adlerian Psychology, the American Society of Group Psychotherapy and Psychodrama, the American Psychological Association, and other professional organizations.

GUILT FEELINGS:
WHAT DO THEY ACCOMPLISH?

Joseph L. Hart

Many of us suffer emotional pain or discomfort because of guilt feelings. It seems that severe cases of scrupulosity have greatly diminished in recent years, but people still experience the agony that comes from intense feelings of guilt. In a recent issue of the *Bulletin of The National Guild of Catholic Psychiatrists,*[1] for example, the lead article is "Understanding Guilt" by Michael Cavanagh; and in the same issue Bernard Tyrrell also discusses the guilt problematic in "Christotherapy: A Concrete Instance of a Christian Psychotherapy." Clinical experience justifies this concern, as the clinician is frequently confronted by

1. Michael E. Cavanagh, "Understanding Guilt," *Bulletin of the National Guild of Catholic Psychiatrists* 23 (1977): 11-18.

clients—lay, religious, and clergy—who are tormented by continuing guilt feelings. The fact that they are sometimes "disguised" as addictions, indecisiveness, overdriven needs, and other compensations, as Cavanagh points out,[2] only compounds the question. Our symposium on guilt and the publication of this book indicate the concern of clergy and religious regarding the phenomena of guilt and guilt feelings.

INTRODUCTION

The intention of this article is to present a perspective on guilt feelings not usually referred to by most writers on the subject. An understanding of the dynamics described below helps diminish the intensity of the feelings—provided the reader is able to laugh at himself or herself.

The article deals with the origins of guilt feelings and their use to help maintain one's idealized self-image by fostering feelings of nobility toward oneself. In addition, the article discusses how we use guilt feelings to give ourselves permission to continue doing a forbidden act, to wrest approval from others, to indulge in self-punishment, and to serve as "life preservers" when we anticipate rejections from others. Finally, the article concludes with the suggestion that what we usually regard as "guilt feelings" are really not feelings of guilt as such but are better explained by other dynamics.

Guilt feelings are inflicted on the person suffering them by the person himself or herself. This simple and obvious statement has important consequences: if persons create their own guilt feelings, if such feelings do not happen to them the way a rainstorm happens to the land, then why

---

2. Ibid., p. 13.

have them? They must serve a fairly important purpose for someone to have and to keep when they cause so much discomfort. If we give guilt feelings to ourselves—"manufacture" them, so to speak—the advantages of having them must outweigh the pain and mental anguish accompanying them. Although I may not be fully aware or conscious of the idea, only *I* can make *my* feelings; no one can create them for me. Someone else may help lay the groundwork or provide the occasion by accusations or criticisms, but only *I* can make my feelings. Why, then, have guilt feelings?

MAINTAINING ONE'S SELF-IMAGE

I believe that, more times than not, we develop guilt feelings to help us keep our idealized self-image intact. It is psychologically important to maintain one's self-image to help provide a sense of personal continuity. We feel secure when we look on ourselves as being basically the same person we were yesterday, last year, twenty years ago, and so on. Our basic character, remaining the same from early years onward, results in an individual's unique attitudes toward one's self, toward others, and toward the demands of life itself. These attitudes remain constant and pervasive throughout life and are often referred to as a person's "life-style" or the "script" one has written for oneself. The idealized self-image is our attitude toward ourself at our best (that we really *are* what we "should" be), and how we like to keep this image in the forefront!

Most of us like to think of ourselves as fairly decent individuals, and any inappropriate behavior on our part attacks that self-image. We are vulnerable to exaggerated feelings of inferiority when that idealized self-image is so attacked by our behavior; then guilt feelings help *lessen* the consequent feelings of inferiority. We are not aware of the dynamics used at the time, but our guilt feelings help restore the somewhat battered self-image, as the following will indicate.

When I have guilt feelings, I become, *on one hand,* the miserable *culprit* who committed those acts for which I feel guilty; but, *on the other hand,* I am the condemning *judge* who is absolutely against those acts. I can then feel good about my noble spirit expressing itself in the role of the judge condemning bad acts! The endangered self-image is protected as the actions of the culprit are judged—the inferior criminal is condemned by the superior judge, both the same person.

In this way guilt feelings serve a purpose for me despite the discomfort of pain that accompanies them. They are maintained because of this purpose, and we are usually not aware of how the psychological gymnastics involved work to our advantage. However, these guilt feelings do help keep the idealized self-image intact because they imply the "goodness" of the judge vis-à-vis the misbehaving culprit.

In these cases another gain is frequently hoped for—that others will judge me for the noble spirit expressed in my guilt feelings rather than for my actual behavior (or at least the expression of guilt will be a mitigating circumstance in my favor). I condemn the very thing I do—and this is a lofty judgment—and hope to impress those around me that my heart is against the dastardly deed. If I succeed, if others think well of me, it is then easier for me to keep that idealized self-image intact.

GUILT AND GUILT FEELINGS—A DISTINCTION

An important distinction must be made here. In this perspective on guilt feelings, there is a vast difference between real guilt and guilt feelings. Real guilt leads to change. With guilt feelings, the same behavior continues. When we do something that violates our conscience, we experience guilt; and there may even be a temporary uncomfortable feeling before we correct the mistake, eliminate the behavior, or do whatever is necessary to bring our conduct in line with our conscience. However, the neurotic-like guilt feelings, referred to in this article and experienced by so many of us, are really *pretensions* of good intentions which we do not have but which permit us to continue doing the same thing. The pretension of good intentions helps keep the idealized self-image intact! ("After all, if I'm this upset about it, I can't be all that bad!")

True guilt leads to action. If I leave a restaurant and realize I inadvertently short-changed the waiter $10.00, I will experience guilt. If I return and pay the $10.00 I owe, there will be no guilt feelings. If I keep the $10.00, I will have guilt feelings because I do not want to think of myself as a dishonest person, cheating a working man. The guilt feelings help me keep the good idea of myself intact—they are saying I must be a fairly decent sort of person, after all, if I feel this bad about what I did. Adler saw this dynamic at work when he was treating an adolescent who had intense guilt feelings about masturbation. Adler told the young person: "Either masturbate or feel guilty. Don't do both, it's too much trouble."[3] He saw guilt feelings as

3. Kurt A. Adler, M.D. From papers presented at the American Society of Adlerian Psychology Convention held in Chicago, May 1977. The author gratefully acknowledges Dr. Adler's clinical observations on guilt and guilt feelings that have been incorporated in this article.

pretensions of good intentions that the person does not really have but which permit the same behavior to continue. Guilt leads to change, whereas guilt feelings permit the behavior to continue. Some religious clients find the above dynamic difficult to apply to themselves in the areas of sexuality. They may, for example, have guilt feelings about masturbation; and when asked: "Why don't you stop and so avoid the uncomfortable guilt feelings?" they say, "I can't." It is then pointed out that if they "can't," they are not responsible and there is no guilt because we are answerable only for our decisions and not for compulsive activities not chosen. Frequently, such an exchange is of little benefit to the clients. They prefer to keep the guilt feelings to bolster the idealized self-image because the activity has been labeled as objectively wrong.

GUILT FEELINGS AND FORGIVENESS

The guilt feelings discussed in this article, while painful, are useful or "purposeful" to their owners. Such feelings promote that sense of nobility mentioned above, and they may help win "mercy" from others' judgments. The owners use them to allow the questionable behavior to continue while they keep the idealized self-image intact. However, guilt feelings bring other benefits. One advantage pertains to the very "religious" persons who do not forgive themselves their sins even though they have received absolution. Thus the persons can think of self as having higher religious morals or principles than those of others, including the priest who gave absolution. In fact, these persons even imply they are superior to God—*He* may have forgiven them, but they have not forgiven themselves; *their* standards are higher. That a person can so think despite Jesus' teaching on forgiveness and the church's teachings on the sacraments points out the powerful advantages neurotic guilt feelings can have for one's psychological life. Jesus invites us to think of His Father—our Father—in the way the father of the prodigal son is portrayed in the parable—loving and forgiving (Lk. 15:11-32). Moreover, the prodigal son did not have to have guilt feelings to win his father's love; in fact, in the parable *the prodigal son did not even have to say, "I'm sorry!"* to win his father's forgiveness. The father expressed his unconditional love as soon as he saw and greeted the boy.

GUILT FEELINGS AND SELF-ACCEPTANCE

These neurotic-like guilt feelings also provide a way of self-punishment. The desire to be punished is really the desire to be accepted, and self-punishment is a mistaken way of attaining self-acceptance. This desire is another reason that guilt feelings will be sustained despite their uncomfortableness. The dynamics begin in childhood. A youngster's misdeed is met with parental condemnation and rejection; the youngster can not tolerate rejection and quickly learns that punishment for the misdeed "cancels out" the crime and rejection. Punishment soon equals acceptance in the youngster's mind as the crime is atoned for; the debt is settled and the scales of justice are balanced. Many children learn to play the part of the disapproving and punishing elders toward the forbidden behavior, and thus the groundwork is laid for guilt feelings as self-punishment in later years. (A mother in a family counseling group told of coming upon her young daughter taking pieces of candy from a candy dish, aware that this act was a "no-no." After taking each piece, the child would slap her wrist and scold herself—before taking another piece!) When neurotic guilt feelings fulfill the need for self-punishment with its concomitant but disguised feeling of self-acceptance, the idealized self-image is, once again, maintained.

Another reason for maintaining guilt feelings is similar to the one just described; I call it "getting it off the hook." As youngsters we quickly learned that a "proper" attitude of guilt following a misdeed generally softened our parents' hearts so that we received a smaller punishment or experienced less rejection. The "Please don't hit me—I'm sorry!" became a plea for exemption from punishment but *with* acceptance because of our "noble" attitude of guilt. We learned that an expression of guilt pays off, and in later life we do not easily discard something as useful as that knowledge. It becomes part of our repertoire, and even as adults we realize that guilt feelings can be an unconscious device to win acceptance. These feelings are like a life preserver as they rescue us from the sinking feeling of rejection by others and the resultant sense of inferiority.

CONVENTIONAL EXPRESSIONS

There are, of course, expressions of guilt feelings that are mere convention. In these instances, the guilt feelings cause little, if any, uncomfortableness. Apologies are an example. The "I'm sorry for being late" when we are not sorry (and even intended to be late) is merely a request for tolerance from others by our expressing good intentions we really do not have. The feeling of guilt implied in the apology, "I'm sorry," is preferred to being on time. A similar but more devastating ploy is one's saying, "I'm sorry if this hurts your feelings, but . . . ,'' and then proceeding to demolish the person. The guilt feelings implied in the ''I'm sorry'' are not real but, like armor, are designed to protect the speaker from an attack or counterattack. These expressions are examples of our conventional ways of speaking and are not the neurotic-like guilt feelings referred to in this article.

CONCLUSION

I would now like to invite the reader to consider that the expression ''guilt feelings'' is a misnomer and that it would be more accurate to describe these sensations as exaggerated feelings of inferiority. Guilt implies an offense against God, neighbor, or self, and can usually be alleviated by cessation of the offense and/or reparation. When such a change takes place, there is no need for guilt feelings. The feelings frequently labeled guilt feelings, usually long lasting and pervasive, are really indications that the persons believe themselves inferior. They have judged themselves as not having maintained or reached the high standards they believe they ''should'' have reached. These high standards usually come from someone else, a parent or teacher, for example. The person believes these standards ''should'' be his or her own, but they are not; they have not been truly assimilated or internalized by the individual concerned and so remain outside the personal value system. However, these standards do remain on the periphery of the person's consciousness because the individual believes they ''should'' be his or her own.

An example may help. A client, a nun in an active community, tortured herself for years with what she called guilt feelings because of the way she acted toward her mother.

In fact, her mother, a dominating and possessive person who never "let go" of her daughter and who was never satisfied with the attention Sister gave her, tried to manipulate the daughter by laying guilt trips on her. She felt that Sister never gave her enough attention, visited her infrequently, etc. In the course of therapy, it became clear to Sister that she had not made mother's value system her own in this area but that she thought she "should" have. She therefore felt inferior by not reaching the artificially high standards she had unconsciously set for herself—that of pleasing mother and meeting mother's expectations. Because she did not—in fact, could not—reach this standard, she felt inferior and labeled this devastating feeling of inferiority as guilt feelings; the "good" daughter was not doing what mother wanted! When Sister became aware of what she was really doing, she was able to decide not only by what criteria or yardstick she would measure her behavior but also how she would evaluate her own life. When she adopted realistic standards—realistic because they were *hers* and not based on the "shoulds" of others—the erroneous feelings of inferiority diminished.

The above example is given because it illustrates how inferiority feelings may erroneously be called guilt feelings. This error happens when individuals fail to meet a standard or set of standards they believe "should" be theirs, and consequently feel inferior toward themselves for not doing so. If the feelings were recognized as inferiority feelings instead of guilt feelings, the persons would be able to reevaluate the standards involved and change those they wish to change. They would have more freedom in judging themselves. They would have more freedom as persons.

SUMMARY

This article has examined several of the uses neurotic-like guilt feelings achieve for their creators. It is hoped that an increased understanding of these dynamics will help to bring them under control, as we are better able to handle our reactions when we are aware of what they accomplish for us. If we can laugh at ourselves—or at least smile inwardly—we can objectify the dynamics, see more clearly what they achieve for us, and so lessen or eliminate them. In this case, guilt feelings would be lessened as we become freer to change either the behavior that brings on the experience of guilt or the criteria that are bringing on the exaggerated feelings of inferiority.

Ed Franasiak, Ph.D., is a psychotherapist and assistant director of the House of Affirmation in Montara, California. He studied at St. Bonaventure University, Olean, New York; Assumption College, Worcester, Massachusetts; and the International Graduate School of Behavioral Science in Switzerland. He received his master's degree in psychology from Boston College and his doctoral degree in clinical psychology from the Psychological Studies Institute, Palo Alto, California. He is a member of the American Psychological Association and the California State Psychological Association.

WHEN ENOUGH IS NOT ENOUGH: AFFIRMED SUFFICIENCY AND GUILT

E. J. Franasiak

How often have you had the feeling that what you did, said, or felt was not "enough"? Recall when your parents or teachers communicated to you that as a young person you did not measure up to the degree you were "supposed to." Or recall when a member of your community, a student in your class, or a patient in the hospital expressed with hostility that you somehow did not make it—did not meet his needs adequately or somehow wronged or harmed him.

Recall such experiences, and you are recalling times when you more than likely felt guilty. If, in fact, you understood and acknowledged that the person filing the complaint about you or your behavior was being honest with you, felt you were wrong, and admitted the wrong, you became more conscious of your human imperfection. You experienced guilt in a useful and healthy way. If, on the other hand, you became depressed and deflated in your sense of esteem, were tempted never to speak to that person again, or would never teach or preach or whatever again, it is likely you denied the other. Most importantly, you denied yourself and more than likely compounded your own neurotic guilt.

Guilt is a fact and experience of every human life. There is no escaping it. We are faced with it every moment of our lives, as it is a fact of our humanness, a factor of the human condition, and a means toward increasing our awareness and acceptance of ourselves and of others. When men and women live together, work together, play and pray together, they will experience, in the daily, concrete moment, feelings of guilt. They will experience guilt for being too slow or too fast, working too hard, or not hard enough; feeling too much or too little; talking too much or being too quiet; taking too much or not giving enough; being overly sensitive or overly insensitive, etc. It is not necessarily in the serious transgressions that people experience guilt. Rather, fellow members in community, colleagues, and friends daily point out hurts and angers, pains and insensitivities that cause guilt. In short, daily life is full of experiences of guilt because through our commitments to people, ideals, and work situations, there are expectations of us—expectations of what "should be done" and how it "ought to be done."

What is guilt? A simple definition is used here. Guilt is a felt sense of tension or conscience-pain accompanied by the thought that I have been wrong or have wronged the other. It is feeling that I as a person have been inadequate, insufficient, or "not enough" in my relationships to the other person, to my work, or to my environment.

An experience of my inadequacy and lack of perfection can be a deep and personal encounter with the existential reality of my humanity. Expressed another way, it is an experience that I have been created in the image and likeness of God, *but I am not God.* When accompanied by genuine contrition, guilt experiences lead to further growth, acknowledgment of human imperfection, consciousness and acceptance of such imperfection with honesty and integrity. Equally important is our need to experience ourselves as adequate, sufficient, and enough: to be right, to be justified, to be proper—in short, guiltless, at least to some degree.

For some men and women, daily experiences of insufficiency do not lead to growth, for they are already trapped in the throes of neurotic guilt. For such people, these experiences compound and confirm the torment of the past in the present. This torment consciously and subconsciously is like an unpaid debt which takes away their internal peace and further threatens an already precarious sense of individuality.

If we reflect on our present culture, we will notice an often blatant consumerism that is popular and fashionable. Every newspaper, magazine, and television program tells us, "You need more . . . ," "Get more out of life by . . . ." Anything conceivably marketable will be marketed. The big question for advertisers is how they can convince the public it needs more. It is the successful advertiser or promoter who ultimately answers this question.

Current "self-help" books of psychology reflect a pursuit of "more": more health; more growth; more and better relationships; more with less, and less with more. We

see widespread psychological, physical, and spiritual consumerism today. Certainly the popularity of this material is
an indication of increasing personal awareness. It is also an
indication of the preoccupation with the insufficient self, a
self motivated by the guilt of knowing it is not enough. It
seeks its sufficiency in external things, activities, or people.
For the person relatively free of gross neurotic conflict, it is
often difficult enough to preserve a sense of adequacy. For
the person caught in neurotic guilt, it is often impossible.

What is neurotic guilt? Neurotic guilt is a confirmation
of already felt insufficiency. It is guilt that is no longer a
felt conscience-pain leading to growth, refinement, or genuine contrition. There are many signs of neurotic guilt.
Most commonly, one experiences a severe self-condemna-
tion which interferes with the mature ability to resolve conflict. Obedience is not exercised out of love but rather is a
defense against feeling anxious. Preoccupation with moral
superiority is evident as one feels morally inferior. Strug-
gles and preoccupations with temptation produce constant
anxiety rather than genuine contrition.

The origins of neurotic guilt lie deep within the human
psyche. They are most often identified as forbidden desires
in the areas of sex and aggression. If we reflect on our own
experiences of recurrent and irrational guilt feelings, we
likely discover that sexuality and aggression are at the
source of such conflicts. I do not intend to go into a
lengthy discussion of these instinct-related fears. However,
suffice it to say that they lie at the core of a person's experience of self as a human being, and they frequently sur-
face as unresolved areas to create neurotic guilt.

We are the product of generations of men and women influenced by a culture which encourages repression and fear of both sex and anger. Stein observes:

> . . . some people—many people—are in the process of growing up, under the tutelage of parents so anxious about instinctual (usually sexual and/or aggressive) behavior that they impose an oppressive instinct-fear on the child, punish his spontaneity and autonomy, and promote deceitful harmony at the price of unconscious self-contempt through superego identification. Because the child experiences the pseudoquality and often brutalization in such value training, his ambivalence and rebellion may be the price he has to pay to maintain his "autonomy" and what sanity he has . . . .
>
> To treat *neurotic* guilt on a confessional, reality basis is to reject the counselee and to identify with his tormentors, internal and historical. It is to deepen his despair, and self-hatred. It is to compound his confusion, minimize his autonomy and maximize either his acquiescent self-abasing conformity or else maximize his rebellious self and other-destructive acting out.[1]

I do not suggest that "passing the buck" or "blaming everything on childhood" is the answer to free and autonomous living. However, what and how we learned as children may have a profound effect on our contemporary life. Frequently, we encounter clients who are hesitant to explore their early childhood development—their feelings about their mother, father, or siblings. They protest that these experiences are in the past, that nothing is to be gained by recrimination, and that parents are not to blame. Yet daily they suffer the torment of neurotic guilt and the

---

1. Edward V. Stein, *Guilt: Theory and Therapy* (Philadelphia, PA: The Westminster Press, 1968), pp. 146-47.

deep perception that they do not measure up or that they are not enough. They are unable to allow another person to affirm them. Such persons often portray their family as near perfect. They cannot bring themselves to acknowledge their parents' imperfections because they would have to come to terms with their own lack of perfection.

It is often these same persons who freely blame church or religious authorities for their troubled present. They have an insatiable need for themselves as well as for their superiors to be perfect. This need is a perpetuation of an insidious cycle of self-destruction and inhuman self-rejection.

It is frequently neurotic guilt that leads us to perceive ourselves as victims of the past, of parents, of institutions, and of people who represent those institutions. We feel that they are to blame. It is their fault that we feel helpless, hopeless, or injured. Indeed, there may be some truth to this feeling. However, blame will satisfy us for only a short duration of time; it will not really make us feel better.

When we blame, we engage in a process called projection. Our lack of experienced sufficiency is placed on some other person or on the environment. It is basically an avoidance of personal responsibility. Jung writes:

> . . . Only the living presence of the eternal images can lead the human psyche to a dignity which makes it morally possible for a man to stand by his own soul, and be convinced that it is worth his while to persevere with it. Only then will he realize that the conflict is *in him,* that the discord and tribulation are his riches, which should not be squandered by attacking others: and that, if fate should exact a debt from him in the form of guilt it is a debt to himself. Then he will recognize the worth

of his psyche, for nobody can owe a debt to a mere nothing.[2]

There is no need to blame anyone. We can accept personal responsibility for all the feelings that we experience. They are not necessarily destructive but may lead to an awareness that we are people limited by time, influenced by culture, and living in a present historical moment.

Guilt has a function in our daily lives. It helps us to become aware of our humanness and can link us to our growth and development in a very authentic way. It keeps us reality oriented. It enables us to experience ourselves as men and women genuinely involved in a life-long task of psychological and spiritual growth and refinement. It functions for us as a warning against our tendency to become insensitive or ego-inflated. It is there to remind us simply and effectively that we are human. It can become a gentle and rhythmic experience of conscience.

Affirmed sufficiency involves my own experience in the concrete lived moment as being enough for the purpose. I am a creature reflective of God's love and goodness, and I satisfy this purpose in my created being. In short, I am enough in His creation.

Guilt is a necessary and unavoidable function of living as an affirmed, sufficient human being. It is there as a reminder of the life-long task of realizing psychological and spiritual affirmation. In describing affirmation, Fr. Kane writes:

. . . affirmation reflects the goodness of a person to himself. You are good because you are you; because you

---

2. Carl G. Jung, *Collected Works,* vol. 14 (Princeton, NJ: Princeton University Press, 1959), pp. 363-64.

have great worth being your unique self. You are God's Creation! Good, not primarily because you have done anything, or accomplished a great deal, or proven that you are successful; no, just because you are you![3]

It is enough that we are creatures of God. Nothing spectacular or dramatic needs to be done about life, being good, loving, or dying. What we need is to face our humanity with a gentleness that we usually reserve for our most loved ones. This gentleness opens us to being affirmed by the other, validates us in our sufficiency, and leads us to the conviction that in our being and person we are enough.

---

3. Thomas A. Kane, *Healing Touch of Affirmation* (Whitinsville, MA: Affirmation Books, 1976), p. 23.